Writers and their Work
A critical and bibliographical series

General Editor
Ian Scott-Kilvert

St Helens
College
Library

POETS OF WORLD WAR I

by

JOHN PRESS

PUBLISHED BY
PROFILE BOOKS LTD
WINDSOR, BERKSHIRE, ENGLAND

First published 1983
Profile Books Ltd
Windsor, Berks
© *John Press 1983*

Typeset and Printed by
Unwin Brothers Limited,
The Gresham Press, Old Woking, Surrey,
England

ISBN 0 85383 608 6

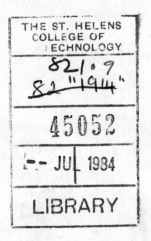

CONTENTS

POETS OF WORLD WAR I

John Press

INTRODUCTION

When Europe went to war in August 1914 it had not witnessed a major conflict since the defeat of Napoleon at Waterloo in 1815, although the war for the liberation of Italy and Bismarck's wars against Denmark, Austria, and France had reminded politicians that violence might be an effective instrument of policy. Britain's only adventure on the continent, the Crimean War, had revealed the criminal incompetence of the army command, the scandalous state of the hospital services as exposed by Florence Nightingale, and the blundering stupidity of military tactics, seen at its most notorious in the charge of the Light Brigade. But all that was over fifty years before. A study of the American Civil War might have prepared the men of 1914 for what lay before them: the employment of artillery on a very large scale; the devastation of the countryside; the destruction of towns and the wandering of refugees from homes they had been forced to abandon. Yet nobody would have believed that the particular kind of savagery endured in the United States in the 1860's would have marked a conflict between the chivalrous professional armies of Europe fifty years later.

Leonard Woolf describes how he walked over the Sussex Downs in the summer of 1914 and how they looked almost as if unchanged since Domesday. World War I was to transform far more than the landscape of Sussex and of the other English counties. The face of the world was changed and, together with the millions who perished on the battlefields or in the influenza epidemic after the war, the civilization of Europe died. The pages that follow record how some English poets fought in the trenches and wrote poems by which they are remembered.

Many of the older poets, who were well over military age, felt the impulse to write patriotic verse about the war. It is better not to quote Sir William Watson's lines about Germany or his address to the Kaiser, but to remark only that he sank to depths of vulgarity and hysteria unplumbed by any other poet in both world wars. Thomas Hardy's 'Men Who March Away' is on a different level of achievement, but it moves with an uncharacteristic jaunty religious fervor that has not worn well. Charles Sorley, a great admirer of Hardy, believed that one line of the poem 'Victory crowns the just' was the worst Hardy had ever written.

Rudyard Kipling (1865–1936) summoned his fellow countrymen to brace themselves for the coming struggle and to gird themselves for sacrifice. 'For All We Have and Are' is an accomplished call to arms, an attempt to stiffen the sinews and to strengthen the will. Kipling warns all patriots that 'The Hun is at the gate,' adroitly seizing on the Kaiser's admonition to his troops at the time of the Boxer rebellion that they should behave like the ancient Huns. Kipling's poems on the war are varied in mood and theme; some are diatribes against politicians who hid the truth before the war and sent men ill-equipped into battle after war had come. He also wrote some memorable epigrams, including one on a soldier executed for cowardice, toward whom he shows an unexpected compassion. Under most of his wartime poems one can detect anger and grief at the death in action of his beloved son.

Unlike Kipling, who was well attuned to the mood of the public, A. E. Housman (1859–1936) caused some offence by his tribute to the regular army, which fought with such courage in the early days of the war and saved the Allies from defeat. People objected to the title of his poem 'Epitaph on an Army of Mercenaries,' on the grounds that it was an insult to a heroic body of men, even though the word 'mercenaries' was an accurate description

of their calling. Nor did the pious relish the poem's last
two lines:

What God abandoned, these defended,
And saved the sum of things for pay.

Today one admires the laconic precision of the phrasing,
the lapidary force of the encomium bestowed by
Housman on men who practised two of the virtues he
most cherished: stoical courage and devotion to duty.

One should pay a brief tribute to Ford Madox Ford
(1873–1939), who insisted on joining the army and who
fought in the trenches, even though over-age. It is true
that he was probably more of a menace to his military
superiors than to the Germans, and that he had enlisted
partly to get away from his mistress, Violet Hunt, who
was proving even more tiresome than his wife. Never-
theless, it was a gallant gesture, and although Ford was
not a very good poet, his 'Antwerp' is an interesting
example of an attempt to adapt and to enlarge imagistic
technique for the purpose of describing war without
emotion. The Belgian, with a smoking gun, is an
uncomely man in an ugly tunic, and when he is killed he
'lies, an unsightly lump on the sodden grass.' As late as
November 1917, T. S. Eliot described 'Antwerp' as 'the
only good poem I have met with on the subject of the
war', which makes one wonder what poems about the war
Eliot had read.

'For the Fallen' by Laurence Binyon (1869–1943) is
probably familiar to more people than any other poem of
World War I. It is so widely known because it is
frequently declaimed at memorial services, including
services in memory of those who died in the Falkland
Islands in 1982. The poem has a solemn, liturgical quality
that commends it to those mourning their dead, and since
it is free of any tincture of Christian devotion, it appeals
to those who want religious dignity without Christian
dogma:

They shall grow not old, as we that are left grow old:
Age shall not weary them, nor the years condemn.
At the going down of the sun and in the morning
We will remember them.   (st.4)

9

Although there is no warrant in the text, congregations habitually supplement the words of the officiating clergyman by intoning a repetition of the last line: 'We will remember them.' The poem of an individual poet is transformed into a communal liturgical rite. None of Binyon's subsequent poems attained anything like the popularity of 'For the Fallen.' Halfway through World War II Binyon wrote a poem called 'The Burning of the Leaves,' which is concerned with the necessity of laying aside all that is ended and done. It may not be fanciful to suppose that he was looking back to the previous war and drawing courage from the experience of 1914–1918 when he achieved the mingled doubt and affirmation of the poem's final line, 'Nothing is certain, only the certain spring.'

Most of the younger poets who had begun to make a reputation by 1914 were associated, at least in the minds of poetry readers, with the Georgians or the Imagists, although these were rough and often misleading classifications. D. H. Lawrence, for example, wandered cheerfully between the two camps, glad to win whatever sustenance he could from either group.

There were obvious links between the Georgians and the war poets, mainly because Edward Marsh printed their work in the anthologies with which he followed up his initial *Georgian Poetry 1911-1912*. His editorial labours did much to spread the fame of Rupert Brooke and to make more widely known the work of Siegfried Sassoon and of the largely forgotten but by no means untalented W. W. Gibson. Edmund Blunden and Ivor Gurney had strong affinities with Georgianism; and even Wilfred Owen was proud to be held peer by the Georgians, greatly though he surpassed them in technical mastery and imaginative force.

Imagism, on the other hand, had little influence on the war poetry written between 1914 and 1918. The younger Imagist poets who served in the trenches included Richard Aldington (later famous as a novelist of the war), Herbert Read, and T. E. Hulme, who was killed in 1915, leaving no war poems. Long after the war Herbert Read sought to explain in *The Contrary Experience* (1963) why the aesthetic theories of Imagism were inadequate to explain the 'terrorful and inhuman events' of the conflict. Certainly Aldington's war poems, though well constructed, are too decorative and remote to move us greatly. Perhaps his best war poem is 'Sunsets,' the first stanza of which can be read simply as an impressionistic evocation of the sky at evening:

The whole body of evening
Is torn into scarlet
Slashed and gouged and seared
Into crimson,
And hung ironically
With garlands of mist.

(1-6)

It is only after reading the second stanza that one understands the sinister import of the first, in which the bloody violence of war is mirrored upon the canvas of the natural world:

And the wind
Blowing over London from Flanders
Has a bitter taste.

(7-9)

Ezra Pound alone among the Imagists found adequate expression for the inner meaning of the war, in *Hugh Selwyn Mauberley*; but that poem lies outside the scope of this essay, since it was written by a man who, though living in England, was a civilian and an American.

Just as the avant-garde poetry of the immediate pre-war years exerted only a marginal influence on the war poets, so the poetry of 1914–1918 barely affected the Modernist movement of the 1920's. Eliot, Pound, and W. B. Yeats seem to have learned nothing even from Owen and Isaac Rosenberg; and although W. H. Auden and the poets of the 1930's professed a deep reverence for Owen, they assimilated little of his achievement except a few technical devices and a tendency to invoke pity as an emotional gesture. It was left to the poets of World War II to discover that certain poems written between 1914

11

and 1918 gave imaginative shape to unchanging truths about the nature of war and of human life.

MORNING HEROES

Whatever might be said against the landed aristocracy and other members of the British ruling classes in 1914, nobody could gainsay their physical courage. The main fear of the young men among them was that the war might be over by Christmas, thus preventing them from killing Germans. Almost all of them had been educated at public schools, where they had absorbed the codes of honour and duty that governed all who grew up there. The poems of Henry Newbolt (1862–1938), though written mainly during the 1880's and 1890's, still expressed the ethics of the public schools. Indeed, Newbolt in 1914 had not felt it necessary to write any new poems: he merely published a collection of his earlier work, of which 70,000 copies were sold. Poems such as 'Vitaï Lampada' may nowadays seem ludicrous, but young officers in 1914 accepted the injunction, 'Play up! play up! and play the game!' Many of these young officers, most of whom were in no sense professional poets, wrote poems that recorded their experience of combat during the period of the war that ran from August 1914 to the end of June 1916, the eve of the Battle of the Somme. After that the world became darker: the experiences, terrifying but sometimes joyful, of Julian Grenfell and Charles Sorley were replaced by the purgatorial twilight in which Sassoon, Owen, and Rosenberg found themselves.

Raymond Asquith (1878–1916), eldest son of the prime minister, practised at the bar after a career of exceptional brilliance at Oxford. He left no war poems and indeed was not a poet, although he wrote extremely skilful parodies and pastiches. He deserves to be remembered for his parody of Kipling's jingoistic 'Soldiers of the Queen,' which begins:

The sun like a Bishop's bottom
Rosy and round and hot.....

He was typical of his class and his generation in that he volunteered for military service when there was no pressure on him to do so; rejected a safe job as a staff officer for the danger and discomfort of the trenches; and died with courage and composure on the Somme in September 1916, during what the divisional commander called 'the greatest of all the war achievements of the Brigade of Guards.'

Herbert Asquith (1881–1947), Raymond's younger brother, managed to go through the war from beginning to end unscathed. He is remembered chiefly for a competent though old-fashioned and conventional sonnet, 'The Volunteer,' about a city clerk who is afraid that he will never break a lance in life's tournament. He volunteers, is killed and lies content. This poem, with its imagery drawn from medieval knight errantry, is typical in its loftiness and total divorce from reality, of the mood in which many young men went to war in 1914. This is not invalidated by the fact that Herbert Asquith wrote 'The Volunteer' in 1912.

One of the closest friends of the Asquiths was Julian Grenfell (1888–1915). His father, William Grenfell, a remarkable athlete, was created Lord Desborough in 1905; his mother, 'Etty,' was probably the most celebrated hostess of her day. Before he was two he had displayed his vigorous enjoyment of killing: 'Determined to kill a mouse. Hammer it with a hammer' (Mosley, *Julian Grenfell*, p. 13). He was a man of considerable intelligence, educated at Eton and Balliol, who in 1909 collected but did not publish a book of essays on social and political themes that his strong-minded mother and her friends heartily disliked. He received a commission in the Royal Dragoons in 1910, having passed first among all university graduate entrants to the army. After service in India and then in South Africa, Grenfell planned to give up his army career so that he might devote himself to painting. Etty, with whom his relations were always complex, mocked him and incited her circle of friends to join in the mockery. He capitulated.

In October 1914 Grenfell sailed for France. Although

he had never enjoyed the mass slaughter that had characterized Edwardian and Georgian shooting parties, Grenfell had always loved solitary killing, because it represented a link with the earth and furthered his pursuit of primitive things. He perfected a technique that enabled him to stalk Germans after dark, to creep close to them and then shoot them. In mid-November he shot a German on each of two successive evenings, for which he was awarded the Distinguished Service Order. When he went home on leave he made an entry in his game book to the effect that on 16 and 17 November 1914 he had bagged a Pomeranian.

Grenfell's attitude to the war was unambiguous: it is to his credit that he did not drape his naked ferocity in sanctimonious moralizing. He was a killer from the egg, describing war as all the most wonderful *fun*. More sinister is his verdict on the life that he was leading:

I have never, never felt so well, or so happy, or enjoyed anything so much. It just suits my stolid health, and stolid nerves, and barbaric disposition. The fighting – excitement vitalises every-thing, every sight and word and action. One loves one's fellow-man so much more when one is bent on killing him.

(Julian Grenfell, p.241)

Yet he was not devoid of human feelings. After a passage in a letter from Flanders written in October 1914: 'I *adore* war. It is like a big picnic without the objectlessness of a picnic' (p. 239) – Grenfell goes on to express his sense of pity at the wretchedness of the inhabitants who had been forced to leave their homes.

At the end of January 1915 Grenfell returned to France, taking with him three greyhounds – he had always loved the breed and before the war had written a poem entitled 'To a Black Greyhound.' On 29 April he wrote 'Into Battle,' the poem that is his surest title to immortality. At 4:00 A.M. on 13 May he was grievously wounded, and although his friends believed that his toughness would pull him through, his wounds proved fatal. On his deathbed, presided over by the indomitable Etty, he quoted Phaedra's song from the *Hippolytus* of

Euripides, a play that he had admired since his boyhood. When on 25 May a shaft of sunlight fell across his feet, Grenfell said, 'Phoebus Apollo,' and did not speak again except once to say his father's name. He died on 26 May with a radiant smile on his face.

'Into Battle' is one of those poems by gifted amateurs that have taken their place in the corpus of English poetry. It brings together many of the strands woven into Grenfell's nature: his love of killing that brought him closer to the earth; the sheer exhilaration of battle; a strain of mysticism. At the age of thirteen, during a thunderstorm, he suddenly seemed to realize God, and he became devoted to Saint Thomas à Kempis.

The poem opens with a celebration of the spring, which will enrich the fighting man. Then follows a section in which Grenfell affirms the kinship between the fighting man and the forces of the universe: 'the bright company of Heaven'; the woodland trees; the kestrel and the little owls:

The blackbird sings to him, 'Brother, brother,
    If this be the last song you shall sing,
Sing well, for you may not sing another;
    Brother, sing.'

(st. 6)

Grenfell ends by envisaging the joy of battle, expressing his trust in the Destined Will, and committing himself to the powers of Day and Night.

Another intimate of the Asquith circle was Patrick Shaw-Stewart (1888–1917), whose career at Oxford was only slightly less brilliant than Raymond Asquith's. After leaving Oxford, he joined Baring's Bank, where he rapidly attained a senior position. Soon after the outbreak of war he became a lieutenant-commander in the Royal Naval Division and fought at Gallipoli. He was killed in action in France late in 1917, having refused to quit the field after his ear had been torn off by shrapnel. An untitled poem was found in Shaw-Stewart's copy of Housman's *A Shropshire Lad*, a book whose influence on him it is difficult to overemphasize. The poem begins:

15

I saw a man this morning
Who did not wish to die.

It then considers the fighting in the Dardanelles,
reflecting for a moment on Helen of Troy and
incorporating into the poem a pun on her name that
derives from Euripides. Shaw-Stewart's attainments as a
classical scholar revalled those of Raymond Asquith, and,
like Julian Grenfell, he turned quite naturally in moments
of crisis and fear to the world of classical Greece. He
communes with Achilles, asking him if it was very hard to
die, and the poem concludes on a note of affirmation, in
which the figure of Achilles is invoked:

I will go back this morning
    From Imbros over the sea;
Stand in the trench, Achilles,
    Flame-capped, and shout for me.

(25–26)

Robert Nichols (1893–1944), although now largely
forgotten, was once a name to conjure with, cherished by
the reading public as all that a young heroic poet should
be, and admired by Edward Marsh as one of his favourite
Georgian poets. Marsh was an influential figure, a
cultivated member of the English upper classes, private
secretary to Winston Churchill, a patron of the arts and
editor of the widely read anthology *Georgian Poetry
1911–1912*, the first of five such collections. Although
Nichols' army career was in no way discreditable, he was
invalided home suffering from shell shock and after five
months' treatment in military hospitals received his
discharge. Robert Graves, who did not like Nichols,
thought him almost a phony, perhaps because after leaving
the army he scored a great success with his lectures in the
United States on the war, in spite of having experienced
active service only for what Graves would have regarded
as a ridiculously brief period.

Nichols' wartime poetry, with its mixture of homo-
sexual eroticism and religiosity, has not worn well. Even
among his contemporaries there were those who found
his work distasteful. Douglas Goldring savagely but

justly called 'The Assault' 'a masterpiece of drivel'; and Wilfred Owen regarded him as 'self-concerned and *vaniteux* in his verse' (*Wilfred Owen: Collected Letters*, p. 511). Yet something survives of the romantic vitality and élan that awoke a response in Nichols' first readers. His description of 'Dawn on the Somme' was written during the Battle of the Somme while he was being treated for neurasthenia in a hospital:

Oh, is it mist, or are these companies
Of morning heroes who arise, arise
With thrusting arms, with limbs and hair aglow,
Towards the risen gold, upon whose brow
Burns the gold laurel of all victories,
Hero and heroes' gold, th'invincible Sun?

(7–12)

After the war his reputation faded, although a selection of his poems, *Such Was My Singing*, appeared in 1942, and he edited *An Anthology of War Poetry* in 1943. Some of his lyrical pieces deserve to be remembered, while 'The Sprig of Lime,' a poem of about ninety lines, surpasses in gravity and tenderness everything else that Nichols wrote. It remains one of the neglected masterpieces of our time.

A far more impressive figure than Nichols was Rupert Brooke (1887–1915), for whom Edward Marsh felt deeper affection than for any other Georgian poet. His legendary fame persists to the present day for a variety of reasons. He had many friends of widely different callings, ranging from Virginia Woolf to Geoffrey Keynes, the distinguished surgeon and literary scholar, and Hugh Dalton, Chancellor of the Exchequer in the Labour Government of 1945. In conversations, diaries, memoirs, and letters they united to celebrate Brooke's physical splendour, intellectual power, and literary gifts. The cult of Rupert Brooke still flourishes, given fresh impetus by the revelation that he and Virginia Woolf once bathed naked; and it is possible even now to wax sentimental over the Old Vicarage, at Grantchester, and to get honey for tea in a tea shop in the village.

17

The building of Rupert Brooke into a legend began almost as soon as he was dead, and it is clear that, in part at least, those who fabricated the edifice did so in order to encourage young men to volunteer for the armed forces. Winston Churchill eulogized him as joyous, fearless, and ruled by high, undoubting purpose. Brooke confessed soon after the outbreak of war that the perils of the time and the darkness of the world made him uneasy and vaguely frightened. Nor was he joyous: he was deeply neurotic, especially in his dealings with women. In a letter of August 1912 to Ka Cox, with whom he had a long affair, Brooke confessed his fear that he was incapable of any fruitful sexual relationship, and testified to his self-disgust. He probably never recovered from the nervous breakdown that ended the affair. After he left Tahiti, where he had found brief happiness with a girl called Taatamata, Brooke received a letter from her full of misspellings in French and English, and he 'gulped a good deal.'

Brooke had achieved a reputation as a poet before 1914. He was one of the six people who met for luncheon in Edward Marsh's rooms on 20 September 1912 and planned the genesis of *Georgian Poetry*. He was probably the most valued contributor to the first anthology, *Georgian Poetry 1911-1912*, which appeared before the end of 1912.

Brooke's response to the war, a group of war sonnets, appeared in *New Numbers*, December 1914, without attracting much attention. In September, Brooke had received a commission in the Royal Naval Division, which early in 1915 sailed for the Dardanelles in the hope of striking a decisive blow against the Turks. Before he was able to accomplish anything of note, Brooke contracted blood poisoning caused by a bite from a mosquito or a scorpion. He died in a French military hospital on the Greek island of Scyros on Saint George's Day, 23 April. The firing party at his grave on the island, traditionally associated with Achilles, was commanded by Patrick Shaw-Stewart.

Even before Rupert Brooke's death one of his five war

sonnets had begun to reach a wide audience. On 5 April 1915, Easter Day, the Dean of Saint Paul's, W. R. Inge, had taken as the text for his sermon Isaiah 26:19 – 'Thy dead men shall live, together with my dead body shall they arise. Awake and sing, ye that dwell in dust'. Inge went on to quote one of Brooke's sonnets, 'The Soldier,' remarking that 'the enthusiasm of a pure and elevated patriotism had never found a nobler expression.' Three days after Brooke's death Winston Churchill praised the war sonnets in the *Times*. On 16 June 1915 the sonnets were gathered into *1914 and Other poems*, edited by Edward Marsh. A few months later they were given a separate edition under the title *1914. Five Sonnets*.

Brooke had a gift for the striking phrase and the rhetorical assertion, as the opening lines of three of his sonnets demonstrate:

If I should die, think only this of me:
   That there's some corner of a foreign field
That is for ever England.

('The Soldier')

Blow out, you bugles, over the rich Dead!
   There's none of these so lonely and poor of old,
But, dying, has made us rarer gifts than gold.

('The Dead')

Now, God be thanked who has matched us with His hour,
   And caught our youth, and wakened us from sleeping,
With hand made sure, clear eye, and sharpened power,
   To turn, as swimmers into cleanness leaping,
Glad from a world grown old and cold and weary,
   Leave the sick hearts that honour could not move,
And half-men, and their dirty songs and dreary,
   And all the little emptiness of love!

('Peace')

Yet the sonnets are inadequate, poetically and morally. Even Julian Grenfell had been content to proclaim his love of killing without prating about the cleansing power of war. Nobody since the emotionally disturbed hero of Tennyson's *Maud* (1855), who resolved to plunge into the slaughter of the Crimea, had supposed that war was likely to offer a regenerative experience. Read in the light of what we know about Brooke's psychological difficulties, these sonnets represent the struggle of a highly strung, desperate man to escape from the emotional problems in which he lay trapped. There was a conscious drive toward simplification and self-sacrifice, a barely conscious drifting toward death.

It is significant that three of his contemporaries, all poets who died in battle, were unimpressed by Brooke's sonnets. In a letter to his mother dated 28 November 1914, Charles Sorley remarks that Brooke 'is far too obsessed with his own sacrifice, regarding the going to war of himself (and others) as a highly intense, remarkable and sacrificial exploit. . . . He has clothed his attitude in fine words; but he has taken the sentimental attitude' (*Letters*, p. 263). Isaac Rosenberg, who was admittedly jealous of Edward Marsh's devotion to Brooke and to his memory, refers in a letter to Mrs. Cohen, probably written at midsummer 1915, to the commonplace phrases in Brooke's 'begloried sonnets' (*Collected Works*, p. 237). Rosenberg thought that his 'Clouds' was a magnificent poem, and, in a letter to Sydney Schiff dating from about August 1916, he singles out for praise Brooke's 'Town and Country,' but remarks of his other poems that 'they remind me too much of flag days' (*Isaac Rosenberg 1890–1918: Catalogue with Letters,* p. 16). Edward Thomas, in a letter to Robert Frost of 19 October 1916, while acknowledging that Brooke had 'succeeded in being youthful and yet intelligible and interesting (not only pathologically) more than most poets since Shelley,' passes a severe judgment on him: 'He was a rhetorician, dressing things up better than needed. And I suspect he knew only too well both what he was after and what he achieved' (*Rupert Brooke: A Biography*, by Christopher Hassell, p. 502).

It would be ungenerous to conclude on a sour note. When Brooke encountered the reality of war in the retreat from Antwerp in late 1914 he was moved to pity by the spectacle of refugees. In the 'Fragment' written on his troopship in April 1915 he describes how, after dark, he remains on deck, watching his friends, unobserved by them. The poem is infused with a profound sadness, an awareness of human fragility. It is worlds away from the mood of the sonnets. Brooke's reaction to Dean Inge's sermon evinces something of his old irony and good sense. When he lay dying, his friend Denis Browne came to his cabin to talk about the Dean's sermon, of which Brooke already knew, having received a newspaper clipping from Marsh. The clipping contained Inge's reservation about 'The Soldier': 'And yet it fell somewhat short of Isaiah's vision and still more of the Christian hope.' Brooke murmured his regret that the Dean didn't think him quite as good as Isaiah. They were his last coherent words.

Charles Hamilton Sorley (1895–1915) had an intense passion for truth:

The voice of our poets and men of letters is finely trained and sweet to hear; it teems with sharp saws and rich sentiments: it is a marvel of delicate technique: it pleases, it flatters, it charms, it soothes: it is a living lie.

(*The Letters with a Chapter of Biography* pp. 37–38)

This passage has sometimes been quoted as Sorley's response to the jingoistic poetry of 1914: in fact, it comes from a paper on John Masefield read to the Literary Society of Marlborough College on 3 November, 1912.

Sorley, was planning to enter Oxford in September 1914, but, after leaving Malborough at the end of 1913, he went to live in Germany in January 1914. He loved Germany, despite his loathing for such evil manifestations as the student corps, with their drunkenness, aggressiveness, and hatred of Jews. Nor did he care for Germany's bigotry and conviction of spiritual superiority. When war broke out he was on a walking tour; he was briefly imprisoned, released, and expelled. As soon as he reached England he applied for a commission.

Sorley was unique among English poets who fought in the war in having an intimate knowledge of Germany. He was in a very small minority of people who detested the tawdry elements in official propaganda, the nauseating humbug preached by journalists and churchmen, whom he stigmatized collectively as Annas and Caiaphas. Even his beloved Hardy's 'Men Who March Away' incurred his displeasure. It is, he says, in a letter of 30 November 1914, 'the most arid poem in *Satires of Circumstance*, besides being untrue of the sentiments of the ranksman going to war: "Victory crowns the just" is the worst line he ever wrote – filched from a leading article in *The Morning Post*' (*Letters*, p. 246).

As early as August 1914 Sorley had grasped the truth that Britain and Germany were engaged in a fratricidal conflict. His sonnet 'To Germany' opens:

You are blind like us. Your hurt no man designed,
And no man claimed the conquest of your land.

The theme of mutual blindness sounds at the end of the octet:

And in each other's dearest ways we stand,
And hiss and hate. And the blind fight the blind.

None of Sorley's poems compares in quality with the finest poetry written during the war: his command of poetic technique was inadequate to bear the charge of his imaginative vision. It is in his superb *Letters*, still available in the original edition of 1919, that one finds the best evidence of his intellectual keenness and searing honesty. Nowhere are these qualities more vigorously exhibited than in Sorley's letter to Arthur Watts of August 1915, describing the excitement of the encounter with the enemy:

...the wail of the exploded bomb and the animal cries of the wounded men. Then death and the horrible thankfulness when one sees that the next man is dead: 'We won't have to *carry* him in under fire, thank God; dragging will do': hauling in of the great resistless body in the dark, the smashed head rattling: the relief, the relief that the thing has ceased to groan: that the bullet or bomb that made the man an animal has now made the animal a corpse. One is hardened by now: purged of all false pity: perhaps more selfish than before. The spiritual and the animal get so much more sharply divided in hours of encounter, taking possession of the body by swift turns. (pp. 305–306)

One of Sorley's best poems is the untitled 'All the hills and vales along,' which owes something in mood to Housman. Written before Sorley had seen active service, it ironically celebrates the fact that the marching men are going to their death, urges them to be joyful, and reminds them that Nature will rejoice at their death as it rejoiced at the death of Socrates and of Christ:

Earth that never doubts nor fears
Earth that knows of death, not tears,
Earth that bore with joyful ease
Hemlock for Socrates,
Earth that blossomed and was glad
'Neath the cross that Christ had,
Shall rejoice and blossom too
When the bullet reaches you.

(st. 3)

Sorley's awareness of mortality and his sense of communion with the dead, which go back to his school days, find expression in two sonnets on death dated 12 June 1915 and in the sonnet 'When you see millions of the mouthless dead,' found among his possessions after his death in action on 13 October 1915. In that final sonnet, as in the June sonnets, one can detect an attempt to resolve a deep ambiguity in his attitude to death. Perhaps it would be truer to say that there coexisted in Sorley a devout belief in the Christian doctrine of the resurrection and a deep subconscious acceptance of the knowledge that death is final.

The final sonnet prefigures in certain ways Owen's apprehension of war as a tragedy in which numberless men meet their death:

When you see millions of the mouthless dead
Across your dreams in pale battalions go ...

(1–2)

The sonnet emphasizes the deadness of the dead, the futility of praise or tears, the remoteness of the dead from the living. It might almost be a rejoinder to Rupert Brooke, whose war sonnets had not commended themselves to Sorley. The final line of the sonnet is difficult to read as other than a denial of immortality: 'Great death has made all his for evermore.'

During the last five months of his life Sorley wrote one or two poems that are no better than the average run of verse in a hymnal or the memorial tributes in a public school magazine. It is not easy to account for this descent into banality of thought and diction; but despite his rebellion against certain aspects of the ethos inculcated at Marlborough, Sorley remained deeply attached to the school and to the downs nearby, where he loved to take his long solitary runs. Perhaps, in the physical and emotional turmoil of the trenches, he at times found solace in reverting to the idiom and the values of his adolescence.

Sorley died so young that his potential as a poet had scarcely begun to develop. He had probably the keenest intelligence and the most admirable nature of all the poets of World War I. The visitor who wishes to enter the chapel at Marlborough, a splendid example of Victorian Gothic, must first pass through the ante-chapel. He will see, affixed to the walls, a number of memorial tablets that honour distinguished sons of the school. Most of them commemorate Victorian admirals, generals, and governors of remote colonies. One is in memory of Charles Hamilton Sorley: it is fitting that it should be there.

Sorley's view of the war was shared by few of those fighting in the trenches. When Siegfried Sassoon and Vivian de Sola Pinto, his platoon commander, first read Sorley's poems in 1916 they could scarcely believe that anybody who had died in action in October 1915 could have taken such an attitude to the war. Young poets continued to write under the influence of Rupert Brooke as late as mid-1916. One such was W. N. Hodgson (1893–1916), an athlete and an exhibitioner[1] of Christ Church, Oxford, who enlisted at the outbreak of the war and won the Military Cross in 1915. His poems, couched as they are in the deplorable idiom of late-nineteenth-

[1]An exhibitioner is the winner of a minor scholarship.

century romanticism, display barely a vestige of talent. However, one poem, 'Before Action,' can still move the reader with its poignant intensity, partly because one knows that it was written by a brave man on 29 June 1916, two days before he died on the first day of the battle of the Somme. The poet moves from a Ruskinian adoration of natural beauty in the opening stanza to a recognition that he has watched

> . . . with uncomprehending eyes
> A hundred of Thy sunsets spill
>   Their fresh and sanguine sacrifice.
>
> (18–20)

Finally the poet faces the knowledge that he

> Ere the sun swings his noonday sword
>   Must say goodbye to all of this;—
> By all delights that I shall miss,
>   Help me to die, O Lord.
>
> (21–24)

The Battle of the Somme ushered in a new and even darker phase of the war. Hitherto it had been just possible to keep up the pretense that there were elements of chivalry in the conflict. At Christmas 1914 in certain parts of the line British and German troops had fraternized, exchanging gifts, singing carols, playing football. The authorities had sternly forbidden the repetition of such gestures and court-martialled Sir Iain Colquhoun and another captain of the Scots Guards for permitting their men to fraternize with the Germans on Christmas Day 1915. A new era of mass slaughter was about to begin. Before the attack on 1 July 1916, Field Marshal Douglas Haig had bombarded the German trenches for a week. Unfortunately, the German dugouts were so deep and well constructed that their machine gunners were able to scramble into position unharmed and mow down the British soldiers as they mounted their assault. The British army lost 60,000 killed and wounded on 1 July, the heaviest casualties it had ever sustained on any one day in its annals. The pattern established on the Somme repeated itself from then on: artillery bombardment, waves of infantrymen assaulting positions defended by heavy concentrations of machine guns, and an advance of a few hundred yards. At Passchendaele the following summer, a new element of horror pervaded the fighting: the sea of mud where rain fell on ground churned up by the British artillery. Not until March 1918 was the stalemate broken, when a German offensive appeared to have won the war. Yet the impetus petered out; on 8 August an Allied counter-offensive broke through the German positions and on 11 November the war was over.

One needs to bear this background in mind when considering the work of Sassoon, Owen and Rosenberg, all of whose best poems were written after the summer of 1916. The public at home still preferred the romantic falsities of Robert Nichols' to the savage truths of Siegfried Sassoon. Nichols' volume *Ardours and Endurances*, published in May 1917, sold more copies than Sassoon's *The Old Huntsman*, which appeared at the same time. But no serious poet could write about the war with the devotional highmindedness that one finds in W. N. Hodgson. He was the last of the morning heroes.

Even before the Somme one or two poets were beginning to make some adequate response to the ghastly realities of the war. Sassoon was writing the first of his trench poems that aimed at presenting an objective picture of life at the front. There was also Arthur Graeme West (1891–1917), who suffered a total revulsion from the war in August 1916, returned to France, and was killed by a bullet in April 1917. His *Diary of a Dead Officer* (1918) records his growing disillusionment. It is mainly prose, with a few poems added, of which the finest is 'Night Patrol,' dated March 1916. West anticipates Sassoon in his determination to record the true visage of war:

> . . . and everywhere the dead.
> Only the dead were always present – present
> As a vile sickly smell of rottenness.
> The rustling stubble and the early grass,
> The slimy pools – the dead men stank through all,
> Pungent and sharp . . .   (19–24)

26

His polemic in 'God! How I Hate You, You Young Cheerful Men,' against those who wrote lyrical poetry in the manner of Rupert Brooke, forms part of his desire to clarify in his own mind the nature of the struggle in which he was enmeshed. In that same poem he makes a more subdued but perhaps more heartfelt protest against the popular concept of God, foreshadowing Wilfred Owen in his speculations about the love of God and the suffering on the battle-field:

> Ah how good God is
> To suffer us be born just now, when youth
> That else would rust, can slake his blade in gore
> Where very God Himself does seem to walk
> The bloody fields of Flanders He so loves.
>
> (34–38)

Even from these brief quotations one observes how far West had travelled from the landscape of the mind portrayed by Grenfell, Brooke, and Shaw-Stewart; how near he was to the no-man's land delineated by Sassoon, Owen, and Rosenberg. Before considering that sombre region, one must turn to the achievement of three men who, belonging to no school, made highly distinctive contributions to the poetry of war.

EDWARD THOMAS, IVOR GURNEY, EDMUND BLUNDEN

In one sense Edward Thomas (1878–1917) can scarcely be called a war poet: he wrote no poems about fighting or about life in the trenches; almost all his poems that refer to the war do so glancingly; and he probably wrote no poems after he had landed in France. Yet in one way Thomas was essentially a war poet: he owed his existence as a poet to the war. He had married very young, and his struggle to support his wife and three children condemned him to a round of ceaseless publishing on a wide variety of subjects – the countryside, Queens of England, English men of letters. Although some of his literary criticism,

27

notably *Algernon Charles Swinburne* (1912) and *Walter Pater* (1913), contains perceptive insights and there are passages worth reading in most of his books, this merely proves his extraordinary stamina and his determination to do honest work for his meagre pay. Being commissioned in the army meant that the worst of his financial worries were over and that he was free of the literary treadmill. Between 3 December 1914 and 24 December 1916, Edward Thomas wrote the body of verse by which he is primarily remembered.

It is not necessary to consider in any detail the debt owed by Thomas to Robert Frost. The strong-minded widows of the two poets turned into a matter of dispute something that Frost and Thomas would have discussed amicably. Frost certainly told Thomas that he should write certain paragraphs of his prose in verse form and keep exactly the same cadence. This may account for the fact that although Thomas's poems are unmistakably poetry they never, even at their most formal, lose touch with the movement of prose.

Thomas's most overt declaration about the war occurs in 'This Is No Case of Petty Right or Wrong,' in which he disclaims all conventional patriotism. When Eleanor Farjeon asked him if he knew what he was fighting for, he picked up a pinch of the earth and said, 'Literally, for this.' So, in the poem, Thomas affirms his irrational love for his country:

I am one in crying, God save England, lest
We lose what never slaves and cattle blessed.
The ages made her that made us from dust.

(21–23)

A subtler, finer poem, 'Tears,' explores Thomas's feeling for his country and tells us even more about his own nature. Although not directly relevant to the war, it gives us more than a hint about his attitude toward the soldiers in the trenches and toward his native land. One April morning he stepped out of 'the double-shadowed Tower' into a courtyard:

28

They were changing guard,
Soldiers in line, young English countrymen,
Fair-haired and ruddy, in white tunics. Drums
And fifes were playing 'The British Grenadiers.'
The men, the music piercing that solitude
And silence, told me truths I had not dreamed,
And have forgotten since their beauty passed.

(12–18)

There are poems by Thomas that seem to have no connection with the war until a phrase arrests one's attention, compelling us to read the poem in a new light. In 'Rain,' one of his most characteristic poems, we encounter a reference to those whose sympathy cannot relieve human suffering, but who lie awake,

Helpless among the living and the dead,
Like a cold water among the broken reeds,
Myriads of broken reeds all still and stiff.

(12–14)

The image of the last line is almost certainly suggested by the victims of slaughter on the battlefields of France and of Flanders.

The war is present even more explicitly in 'The Owl.' As in so many of his poems, Thomas writes here in the first person, describing how hungry, cold, and tired he was, until he had satisfied his needs at an inn. An owl's 'most melancholy cry' leads him away from a preoccupation with his solitary pains into an imaginative sympathy with others:

And salted was my food, and my repose,
Salted and sobered, too, by the bird's voice
Speaking for all who lay under the stars,
Soldiers and poor, unable to rejoice.

(st. 4)

The conjunction of soldiers and poor recalls Isaac Rosenberg's observation that privates in the army are akin to slaves. For Thomas, soldiers are not heroes or our gallant boys in the trenches, but rather men low on the social scale, on a level with the poor. They suffer passively, unable to rejoice.

The four-line poem 'In Memoriam (Easter 1915)' is both a beautiful elegy and a powerful comment on the war:

The flowers left thick at nightfall in the wood
This Eastertide call into mind the men,
Now far from home, who, with their sweethearts, should
Have gathered them and will do never again.

The emphasis falling on 'should' makes us aware that it may be read in two ways: the simple observation that the soldiers would have gathered the flowers had they been home; and the implication that the war, by destroying the dead men, has broken the ritual of courtship, the gathering of flowers that the dead men ought to have performed. Once again Thomas is showing how a tiny incident in a peaceful countryside may help us to grasp the significance of war.

One observes the same kind of strategy in 'As the Team's Head-Brass.' A soldier who has not yet been out to the war is watching a man ploughing a field. Lovers disappear into the wood, and the ploughman stops from time to time to have a word with the soldier. Their conversation veers toward the war: the fallen elm on which the soldier is seated won't be taken away until the war is over; the soldier could spare an arm but would be reluctant to lose a leg; one of the ploughman's mates died on his second day in France. The talk is consequential and casual, yet the poem gradually pieces together a picture of the way in which the war demands and deprives. The poem ends with what is almost certainly something more than a straightforward description of the landscape:

The lovers came out of the wood again:
The horses started and for the last time
I watched the clods crumble and topple over
After the ploughshare and the stumbling team.

(34–37)

The menace hidden in the phrase 'for the last time' may remind the reader that the soldier, like the men who will never again gather the flowers, will perhaps, as he fears, lose not just an arm or a leg in battle, but his head as well.

There is even a hint that the lovers and the age-old relationship between man and the soil are under threat from the destructiveness of war.

Edward Thomas is the quietest, most introspective of all the war poets, but the keenness of his observation and the probing quality of his imagination enable him to penetrate beyond the outer semblance of things into the heart of sadness.

Ivor Gurney (1890–1937) was that rare creature, a poet who was also a composer, equally gifted in the two arts. The son of a Gloucester tailor, he grew up and was educated in the cathedral city that he never ceased to love. His intelligence and his musical gifts augured well for his future, and nobody found it ominous that his fellow schoolboys gave him the nickname of 'Batty Gurney.'

In the autumn of 1911 Gurney won a scholarship to the Royal College of Music, where he showed his precocious skill in 1912, by his setting of five Elizabethan lyrics, a composition that he called 'The Elizas.' In 1912–1913 he began to write poetry, an activity that was not only of value in itself, but also an influence on his music; for Gurney was to set poems by most English poets of merit who flourished during the first two decades of the twentieth century. His joining the army did not put an end to his composition of music or of poetry: in 1916–1917 he achieved what may well be the unique feat of writing five songs while undergoing a spell of duty in the trenches. He sent home to a friend the poems that he had been writing, and in 1917 they appeared under the title *Severn and Somme*, names of the river that he had loved in childhood and the river associated with the terrible fighting that Gurney had known, and in which on 7 April 1917 he was wounded. In September 1917 he was gassed and sent home, then transferred to a mental hospital at Warrington and later to a similar hospital at St. Albans. His military career was over, formally terminating with his discharge in October 1918. There seems to be something mysterious about Gurney's last thirteen months in the army, since little is known about the circumstances of his gassing or of his confinement to the two mental hospitals. By 1919 he had apparently recovered.

From 1919 to 1921 he cut something of a figure at the Royal College of Music and in the literary world of London, a second book of poems, *War's Embers*, having appeared in 1919. Even so, he depended for his survival on a weekly allowance from a fund raised by his teacher Vaughan Williams and by friends. Back in Gloucester, he talked brilliantly and tumultuously, received financial help from Edward Marsh, and grew ever wilder. He was incarcerated in September 1922 at Barnwood House, Gloucester, and in December at the City of London Mental Hospital, Dartford, Kent. There he remained until his death on 26 December 1937, St. Stephen's Day, at a time of year that meant much to him.

Although Gurney's friends never deserted him, the story of his life at Dartford is heartrending. Apart from his bitter resentment at what he believed to be his betrayal by his country, Gurney was tormented by delusions that he was suffering from tortures inflicted from a distance by electricity. He claimed to have composed the works of Shakespeare, Beethoven, and Haydn. It is likely that he enjoyed (if that be the word) periods of lucidity. When in 1937 a friend told him that Oxford University Press was about to publish a collection of his songs, he merely said, 'It is too late.'

The poems written before he finally went mad are mostly acceptable exercises in the pastoral mode and reflections on various aspects of beauty. Two war poems stand out from the rest of those early poems. 'To His Love,' written when Gurney received a false report that his friend F. W. Harvey had died in battle, deploys in the first three stanzas the conventional properties of pastoral elegy – grazing sheep, the small boat on the Severn, the violets from the riverside. The final stanza opens decorously, but suddenly administers a shock:

Cover him, cover him soon!
  And with thick-set
Masses of memorial flowers
  Hide that red wet
  Thing I must somehow forget.   (st. 4)

Calling a dead man a 'red wet/Thing' strikes one with a raw violence, and it is almost as brutal to suggest that one should cover the corpse with masses of flowers partly in tribute and partly to blot it from sight.

Even finer is Gurney's 'Ballad of the Three Spectres,' a poem that somehow captures the spirit of the Border Ballads without lapsing into archaism or pastiche. The first two stanzas may yield some idea of the poem's merit:

As I went up by Ovillers
   In mud and water cold to the knee,
There went three jeering, fleering spectres,
   That walked abreast and talked of me.

The first said, 'Here's a right brave soldier
   That walks the dark unfearingly;
Soon he'll come back on a fine stretcher,
   And laughing for a nice Blighty.

The curt off-rhymes in both stanzas enhance the atmosphere of menace and strangeness, just as it is sinister that one of the apparitions should speak the slang of the trenches, prophesying that the soldier will get a 'nice Blighty' – a wound bad enough to ensure his return to England.

Yet the best of the poems that he wrote during his madness surpass even the most accomplished examples of his early work. One has to face the question of his insanity before turning to consider the poems composed in the asylums, and the evidence is probably inadequate for anybody to reach a verdict. The latest opinion is that he, like his mother, suffered from paranoid schizophrenia. Should this be so, one cannot lay the blame on the war for driving him mad, though the war almost certainly intensified his madness and determined the pattern that it took. Although the power to compose music left him after 1926, he was able to produce a mass of poetry throughout his confinement at Barnwood and at Dartford from 1922 to 1937.

Some of his poems are painful to read. Two long letters in verse to the Metropolitan Police ramble on about his war service and the pain that he is wrongfully enduring.

All the sentences taken separately are logical, but something has gone wrong with the links between them, and gradually one realizes that the writer has lost his reason. A poem written at Barnwood House in December 1922 is far more controlled, despite the anguish that racks the poet as he draws up his indictment. The opening lines of 'To God' are both tragic and comic in a pathetic way. Gurney's first example of God's cruelty toward him is that there are prayers with meals:

Why have You made life so intolerable
And set me between four walls, where I am able
Not to escape meals without prayer, for that is possible
Only by annoying an attendant?

What is so unnerving in the poem is the mixture of factual observation about forced meals, mere delusion about torture by electricity, and the prayer for death:

  Forced meals there have been and electricity
And weakening of sanity by influence
That's dreadful to endure. And there are others
And I am praying for death, death, death.

(9–12)

Gurney's bitter sense of having been betrayed by his country is certainly linked with his insanity, although nobody has explained precisely how. He seems to have felt outraged in that his sufferings during the war had not brought him merited fame. He may also have experienced anger and pity at the recollection of the suffering endured by others who fought. The prime emotion of 'There Is Nothing' is certainly pain at his own betrayal. The poem, dated February 1925, bears the note 'in torture':

Soldier's praise I had earned having suffered soldier's pain,
And the great honour of song in the battle's first gray show—
Honour was bound to me save - mine most dreadfully slain.

(12–14)

During the years at Dartford, Gurney continually reverts to his memories of the war. Some of the poems he wrote on that theme are so lucid that it is hard to believe he was other than sane when he was composing them. They display an unwavering control of mood and of tone as he remembers the killing of comrades or calls to mind with stoical irony those who for a while, until death took them, contrived to beat the system. These poems have no parallel in the work of any other war poet: the voice is Gurney's alone, speaking clearly and with authority from the depths of a mental hospital.

Two poems in particular yield a taste of Gurney's quality. 'The Silent One' begins curtly in the middle of the story:

Who died on the wires, and hung there, one of two—
Who for his hours of life had chattered through
Infinite lovely chatter of Bucks accent:
Yet faced unbroken wires; stepped over, and went
A noble fool, faithful to his stripes – and ended.

It is all there in five lines: the tale of an honest countryman, a loyal NCO, obedient to his orders, who ended up hanging on the barbed wire. Then an officer, with 'a finicking accent,' unlike the Bucks accent of the dead man, politely asks the narrator of the poem if he'd mind crawling through a hole in the wire. The courteous exchange between the officer and the narrator derives its savour from the fact that it is taking place in the middle of the battlefield, where one might expect orders to be rapped out. There is a measure of anger smouldering away in the poem, whose irony points at the upper-class voice of the officer, at God, and at the narrator himself. The apparent casualness hides a cool artistry. The narrator lay down under unbroken wires,

Till the politest voice – a finicking accent, said:
'Do you think you might crawl through there:
    there's a hole'
Darkness, shot at: I smiled, as politely replied—
'I'm afraid not, Sir.' There was no hole no way to
    be seen.
Nothing but chance of death, after tearing of
    clothes
Kept flat, and watched the darkness, hearing bullets
    whizzing—
And thought of music – and swore deep heart's
    deep oaths
(Polite to God) . . .   (9–16)

35

Equally fine is 'The Bohemians,' a portrait of Gurney and his friends, who found army regulations irksome, who wanted to be left alone:

Certain people would not clean their buttons,
Nor polish buckles after latest fashions,
Preferred their hair long, puttees comfortable.

(1–3)

He describes how they never adapted themselves to military ways.

Surprised as ever to find the army capable
Of sounding 'Lights Out' to break a game of Bridge,
As to fear candles would set a barn alight.

(14–16)

Only in the last line of the poem does Gurney move almost imperceptibly from gentle irony into the starkness of an epitaph:

In Artois or Picardy they lie – free of useless fashions.

It is impossible to say just how good a poet Gurney was, because most of his work remains unpublished. Michael Hurd, who has laboured so long and so effectively on the texts of Gurney's poems, reckons that 600 out of his 900 poems have not been published. About 300 are viable, many of them of the highest quality: it is sad to think that such richness lies neglected in the Gurney archive of the Gloucester public library. The cruel mischance that confined him to mental hospitals for the last fifteen years of his life still has the power to obscure his fame.

Edmund Blunden (1896–1974) remains an undervalued poet, partly because even his war poems are often held to be academic and pastoral, especially by those who have not read them. Joining the army early in 1915, he had already published two small collections and was to bring out a third in 1916, *Pastorals*, which was, like the two earlier volumes, devoted to the countryside in time of peace. Yet he was rapidly changing, as he tells us in *War Poets: 1914–1918*:

In May and June 1916, in my notebooks, the grimness of war began to compete as a subject with the pastorals of peace. By

SIEGFRIED SASSOON

Courtesy of Imperial War Museum   *Self portrait*

ISAAC ROSENBERG

JULIAN GRENFELL

Mark Gerson

DAVID JONES

the end of the year, when madness seemed totally to rule the hour, I was almost a poet of the shell-holes, of ruin and of mortification.

(p. 24)

Blunden was awarded the Military Cross and saw as much hard fighting as any other war poet. In Raymond Asquith's letters home, printed in John Jolliffe's *Raymond Asquith: Life and Letters*, one learns that, despite the killing, the pain, the fear, the acute discomfort, and the boredom, there were moments of exaltation and pleasure during the war: the singing of nightingales or the enjoyment of splendid food and drink. Such moments seldom find their way into the poems of the most powerful war poets, such as Sassoon, Owen, or Rosenberg. It is a mark of Blunden's rare honesty and range of sympathies that he can reveal the less dark sides of war:

O how comely it was and how reviving,
When with clay and with death no longer striving
   Down firm roads we came to houses
   With women chattering and green grass thriving.

   Gazed on the mill-sails, heard the church-bell,
   Found an honest glass all manner of riches.

('At Senlis Once,' 1–4; 11–12)

It is typical of Blunden that the first, Miltonic line should lead us not into deep metaphysical speculation but into a remembrance of lesser mercies.

Blunden knows that, in war, innocent relaxation may for an hour or so charm away the ferocity of killing. Both are aspects of war. In 'Concert Party: Busseboom,' the audience, delighted by the entertainment, reluctantly leaves the world of illusion:

We heard another matinée,
   We heard the maniac blast

Of barrage south by Saint Eloi,
   And the red lights flaming there
Called madness: Come, my bonny boy,
   And dance to the latest air.

To this new concert, white we stood;
  Cold certainty held our breath;
While men in the tunnels below Larch Wood
  Were kicking men to death.

(15-24)

Blunden grew up in a Kent village where, as in Leonard
Woolf's Sussex, life still went on much as in the days of
the Domesday Book. Even at school he was a scholar and a
poet, deeply versed in the pastoral tradition of English
poetry. But his own poetry is pastoral not only because of
his literary learning but because he was genuinely a
countryman. The weakness of his verse over the years is
that he tends to retreat into archaism and whimsy, but his
love for the fields and woods that he discovered in France
lends an element of strength and perceptiveness to his war
poetry. He loathes the war because it violates the pieties
of nature no less than the sanctity of man. As early as May
1916 he linked the two in 'Festubert: The Old German
Line':

Sparse mists of moonlight hurt our eyes
With gouged and scourged uncertainties
Of soul and soil in agonies.

(1-3)

One of his most moving poems, 'Report on Experience,'
published in the collection *Near and Far* (1929), takes up
the earlier theme. The good man and the enchanting
Seraphina, 'like one from Eden,' are victims of the war,
which has also devastated a landscape:

I have seen a green country, useful to the race,
Knocked silly with guns and mines, its villages vanished,
Even the last rat and the last kestrel banished—
  God bless us all, this was peculiar grace.

(st. 2)

The poem ends with an affirmation, not of faith as a
Christian would understand it, but of a belief that we live
in an ambiguous universe presided over by a distant God:

Say what you will, our God sees how they run,
These disillusions are His curious proving

That He loves humanity and will go on loving;
  Over there are faith, life, virtue in the sun.

(st. 4)

The war continued to haunt Blunden's imagination. He collected many of his best war poems as a supplement to the prose narrative of *Undertones of War* (1928). One of the finest is a singularly beautiful elegy, 'Their Very Memory,' that reveals Blunden as a master of rhythmical subtlety. The imagery of the poem evokes running water, green valleys, a spring, a fountain, a greenwood, music. Although Blunden's memory of his comrades is fading, it has not wholly vanished:

  When they smiled,
Earth's inferno changed and melted
  Greenwood mild;
Every village where they halted
  Shone with them through square and alley.

(st. 3)

Even when Blunden is not ostensibly writing about the war, it presides over his meditations. His justly admired poem 'The Midnight Skaters,' from *English Poems* (1925), evokes death at watch within the pond's black bed:

What wants he but to catch
  Earth's heedless sons and daughters?
With but a crystal parapet
Between, he has his engines set.

(9–12)

The word 'parapet' intrudes into a tranquil, Wordsworthian scene like an icy wind blowing from no-man's-land.

Even after World War II, the memory of World War I steals into poems far distant in time and place. When Blunden was working in Hong-Kong, the Communists allowed him to visit the Great Wall of China, because he was a poet and because they rightly believed that he would make no political use of his visit. His sonnet 'At the Great Wall of China' is, sadly, one of the few poems of his later years fit to rank with the best of his work. The parapet reappears in the sonnet's octet, more appropriately perhaps than in 'The Midnight Skaters.' We look from a tower and imagine:

Where these few miles to thousands grow, and yet
Ever the one command and genius haunt
Each stairway, sally-port, loop, parapet,
In mute last answer to the invader's vaunt.

(5–8)

It is in the sestet that the memories of Blunden's war loom unmistakably clear:

But I half know at this bleak turret here,
In snow-dimmed moonlight where sure answers quail,
This new-set sentry of a long dear year.

(9–11)

For there are two ghosts at the bleak turret: that of a young Chinese soldier and that of a British sentry on the Ancre or the Somme. They merge insensibly in the mind of an English poet.

Blunden's war poetry is tougher than commonly supposed. Even though he wrote pastoral verse and, at the end of *Undertones of War* (p. 34), called himself 'a harmless young shepherd in a soldier's coat,' he was adopting a strategy that enabled him to confront the war and record what he observed. In old age he went to live in Suffolk at the village of Long Melford with his wife and daughters, wrote a guide to the magnificent church, and composed an obituary for his old friend Siegfried Sassoon, who was, like Blunden, a survivor of the trenches, a holder of the Military Cross, and an honoured poet.

It is time now to consider the work of two men whose view of the war is darker and more tragic than that of the poets so far discussed. (There will not be an account of Wilfred Owen, since he is the subject of a separate essay in this volume.)

SIEGFRIED SASSOON

Siegfried Sassoon (1886-1967), who was born into a rich Jewish family, left Cambridge without taking a degree and in the years before 1914 devoted himself to hunting, cricket, golf, ballet, opera, and evenings at his London club. He also began to develop a taste for literature, bringing out his privately printed collection, *Poems*, in 1906 and *The Daffodil Murderer* in 1913. This poem, which appeared under the pseudonym Saul Kain, was a parody of John Masefield but also a serious attempt to portray the feelings of the poor and the degraded.

Sassoon, who had joined the army on the first day of the war, rapidly acquired a reputation for courage that bordered on the insane. He stood several inches over six feet, and was lean, athletic, and reckless: it is not surprising that this formidable killer acquired the nickname 'Mad Jack.' His poem 'The Kiss,' whatever he may have though of it later, is written in praise of 'Brother Lead and Sister Steel.' In the Somme offensive of July 1916 he fought with such gallantry that he was awarded the Military Cross. But his attitude toward the war had already begun to change.

It is not easy to chart the logical progress of that change, if only because Sassoon lived by generous passion rather than by calm reason. He may have reacted strongly against lectures on 'the spirit of the bayonet,' given at the Fourth Army School at Flixécourt in the spring of 1916, lectures that aroused the disgust of poets as various as Edmund Blunden, Robert Graves, and David Jones.[1] He had begun writing early in 1916 what he himself called genuine trench poems that were the first things of their kind. Further stages in his pilgrimage include meetings at Garsington Manor, Oxfordshire, the home of Philip Morrell, MP, and Lady Ottoline Morrell, with a number of prominent pacifists, including Bertrand Russell; and a spell in hospital after being invalided home with a bullet

---

[1] Robert Graves is the subject of a separate essay in this series. Therefore, there is no discussion of his poetry here. His war poems form only a minor part of his work.

wound in his lung, sustained at the battle of Arras in April 1917, the engagement in which Edward Thomas was killed.

By February 1917 Sassoon was already losing his belief in the war, and in July he made a protest against its needless prolongation. This 'act of wilful defiance of military authority,' as Sassoon described it, rendered him liable to court-martial and imprisonment. Thanks largely to the intervention of Robert Graves, an alternative procedure was followed, and Sassoon, who had meanwhile thrown his Military Cross into the Mersey, agreed to appear before a medical board. Graves testified that Sassoon suffered from hallucinations typical of shell shock and himself burst into tears three times while making his statement. The board dispatched Sassoon to Craiglockhart War Hospital, appointing as his escort Robert Graves, who missed the train that was carrying Sassoon to his destination.

At Craiglockhart the doctors cured Sassoon of whatever illness had prompted him to issue his act of defiance, and he asked for a posting abroad. He arrived in Egypt at the end of February 1918, then moved to France in May. His fighting days came to an end on 13 July 1918, when, on a daylight patrol, he was accidentally shot through the head by a British sentry and sent home to pass the rest of the war in hospital.

Two volumes of poetry, *The Old Huntsman* (1917) and *Counter-Attack* (1918), contain almost all the enduring poems that Sassoon wrote about the war. The judgment that he is primarily a satirist is questionable, but his satirical poems retain to this day their incisiveness and power. In 'They,' Sassoon launches an attack not only on a complacent, stupid bishop but on the apparent subservience of the Anglican church to the state, and on the windy rhetoric that was one of the main civilian contributions to the war:

The Bishop tells us: 'When the boys come back
They will not be the same; for they'll have fought
In a just cause; they lead the last attack
On Anti-Christ.'
(st. 1)

The next stanza contrasts the stale abstractions by which the bishop lives with the raw truths that are the products of war:

'We're none of us the same!' the boys reply.
'For George lost both his legs; and Bill's stone blind;
'Poor Jim's shot through the lungs and like to die;
'And Bert's gone syphilitic; you'll not find
'A chap who's served that hasn't found *some* change.'
And the Bishop said: 'The ways of God are strange.'

(st. 2)

In view of his official and social position, Edward Marsh showed courage when he published the poem: the mention of syphilis was an offence against decorum and an affront to patriotic feeling.

There are moments when Sassoon's rage may seem to be in excess of its object. In January 1917, just before returning to France, Sassoon went to a revue at the Hippodrome in Liverpool and wrote a poem designed to be his farewell to England:

    . . . prancing ranks
Of harlots shrill the chorus, drunk with din;
'We're sure the Kaiser loves our dear old Tanks!'

I'd like to see a Tank come down the stalls,
Lurching to rag-time tunes, or 'Home, sweet Home.'
And there'd be no more jokes in Music-halls
To mock the riddled corpses round Bapaume.

('Blighters,' 2–8)

It is little hard on the inoffensive chorus girls to stigmatize them as harlots, and the audience hardly deserves to be massacred. But Sassoon believed that the ignorance of civilians about what was happening on the battlefield was criminal. Songs in music halls about tanks were blasphemous insults to the troops and to their dead comrades. Viewed in this light, 'Blighters' is a valid testament of justified indignation. Its final line, particularly when spoken aloud, delivers a searing curse on those who thoughtlessly mock the agony of their fellow men.

Some of Sassoon's other satirical poems have become anthology pieces, such as 'Base Details,' 'Glory of

Women,' 'Does It Matter?' 'The General,' and 'Fight to a Finish,' a savage attack on civilians, especially journalists and members of Parliament.

Most of his poems have scarcely any satirical element, but take as their theme trench warfare, presented with an almost brutal realism, although the underlying tenderness aroused by the spectacle of the wounded and the dead redeems what would otherwise be almost intolerable. In 'Attack,' Sassoon, while playing down the worst of the horror, describes what it was like to go over the top:

Lines of grey, muttering faces, masked with fear,
They leave their trenches, going over the top,
While time ticks blank and busy on their wrists,
And hope, with furtive eyes and grappling fists,
Flounders in mud. O Jesus, make it stop!

(9–13)

Some reviewers of *Counter-Attack* condemned Sassoon for his insistence on the ugly aspects of war. In the title poem he portrays as faithfully as a Dutch seventeenth-century painter the contents of a captured trench:

The place was rotten with dead; green clumsy legs
High-booted, sprawled and grovelled along the saps
And trunks, face downward, in the sucking mud,
Wallowed like trodden sandbags, loosely filled;
And naked sodden buttocks, mats of hair
Bulged, clotted heads slept in the plastering slime.
And then the rain began, – the jolly old rain.

(st. 1)

This is no mere catalogue of horrifying items: the dense particularity of the description achieves a sensuous richness. The green legs are ghastly because the adjective suggests both the fertility of spring and the gangrenous texture of the rotting corpses. In a similar way the word 'slept' has associations of repose that are mocked by the way in which the clotted heads sink into the slime. The stanza's last line, with its casual irony, provides a moment's relief from one's scrutiny of the dismembered bodies.

Although Sassoon wrote nothing else so richly complex as 'Counter-Attack,' he produced a number of memorable poems about various aspects of trench warfare. One of the most effective is 'The Rear-Guard,' set in a tunnel under the Hindenburg Line in April 1917 and based on an experience of his own. The narrator, who has not slept for days, is furious when a sleeping figure over whom he stumbles fails to wake up and answer his questions:

Savage, he kicked a soft, unanswering heap,
And flashed his beam across the livid face
Terribly glaring up, whose eyes yet wore
Agony dying hard ten days before;
And fists of fingers clutched a blackening wound.

(st. 3)

Two of Sassoon's poems are unusual in that they are explicitly elegiac. 'To Any Dead Officer' mingles anger, mockery, and compassion, passing from a lament for one particular officer to a fine passage in which Sassoon mourns all who were reported 'wounded and missing':

Next week the bloody Roll of Honour said
    'Wounded and missing' – (That's the thing to do
When lads are left in shell-holes dying slow,
    With nothing but blank sky and wounds that ache,
Moaning for water till they know
    It's night, and then it's not worth while to wake!).

(st. 4)

'To One Who Was With Me in the War,' written in 1926, is not so much a formal elegy as a 'game of ghosts,' in which the poet imagines going back with a fellow officer after the war to 'some redoubt of Time,' where they may relive their experience of the trenches. It is a less urgent, mellower poem than those Sassoon wrote during the war, yet it conveys something of his complex emotions toward that war:

    Round the next bay you'll meet
A drenched platoon-commander; chilled, he drums his feet
On squelching duck-boards; winds his wrist-watch;
    turns his head
And shows you how you looked, – your ten-years-
    vanished face,

Hoping the War will end next week . . .
   What's that you said?

(32–37)

After the war was over Sassoon returned to his old life, combining his sporting interests with literary activity. He became widely known for a series of prose autobiographies that cover his life from the closing years of the nineteenth century to the end of the war. He continued to write poetry during the rest of a long life, happy to employ the diction and the metres of his youth, unswayed by the innovatory techniques of Pound, Eliot, and the Imagists. His poems include gentle satires on, for example, the first performance of Stravinsky's *Rite of Spring* and the destruction of Devonshire House; reminiscences of the war; and explorations of religious and mystical themes. But it is by virtue of thirty or forty poems that delineate the agony of the fighting in the trenches that he holds an honoured place among English poets.

ISAAC ROSENBERG

Isaac Rosenberg (1890–1918) is one of the few Englishmen to have achieved distinction as a poet and a painter. He was born in the East End of London and was the son of Lithuanian Jews who had emigrated to Britain in the 1880's. After leaving school in 1904 he was apprenticed to a firm of art publishers, but chafed at the narrowness of his life. Thanks to the generosity of some Jewish ladies, he was able in October 1911 to enrol at the Slade School, where he met gifted fellow students such as David Bomberg, Mark Gertler, Dora Carrington, Edward Wadsworth, Paul Nash, and Stanley Spencer. He published at his own expense in 1912 a booklet of poems, *Night and Day*, in which he was already expressing his perplexities about the significance of suffering and the nature of God.

On 10 November 1913 Gertler introduced Rosenberg to Edward Marsh at the Café Royal. For the rest of Rosenberg's life Marsh gave him all manner of help, buying his paintings, paying for the publication of his second book of poems, *Youth* (1915), and doing what he could to relieve Rosenberg's difficulties after he had joined the army.

The relationship between a man and his patron is always subject to strains of various kinds, and it must be admitted that Rosenberg and Marsh were seldom in perfect accord. Marsh was a cultivated member of the English upper classes, private secretary to Winston Churchill, a man of conservative taste, editor of the Georgian anthologies, a passionate admirer of Rupert Brooke. It is easy to draw up an indictment of Marsh, pointing at his failure to recognize the genius of Rosenberg; at his exclusion of him from his anthologies, except for a speech from *Moses*; at his inability to admire 'Dead Man's Dump.' It is even held against Marsh that, years after the end of the war, he could still talk of 'poor little Rosenberg.'

Yet Marsh proved a true friend to Rosenberg. It was Marsh who ensured that Rosenberg's mother received from the army the allowance due to her, just as it was Marsh who did all in his power to have Rosenberg moved to safer and less exacting military duties. Despite his failure, to respond to 'Dead Man's Dump,' he took the trouble, before returning the manuscript to Rosenberg, to copy out the poem for fear that it might be lost. Nor did Marsh call him 'poor little Rosenberg' in a spirit of upper-class condescension. Mark Gertler, a poor, working-class, East End, Jewish painter, described Rosenberg affectionately as a 'funny little man.' It is possible to be a poet of the first order and also a poor, funny little man.

In June 1914 Rosenberg visited Cape Town, where he stayed with his married sister, Minnie. He wrote there 'On Receiving News of the War,' a poem that anticipates the end of the old order, a poem of foreboding deeper than any experienced by his compatriots at home. For over a year before the outbreak of war he had been concerned with the need to reject the orthodox male God, and in the late summer of 1914 he was working on his poem entitled 'The Female God,' an exploration of the sexual and the sacred.

Rosenberg went back to England in February 1915, although he could have stayed on in Cape Town indefinitely, especially as he was much in demand as a portrait painter. Apparently he felt that he had reached an emotional and spiritual dead end. But in London things were little better, and in the autumn of 1915 he enlisted in the army, partly to obtain an allowance for his mother and partly, it has been surmised to fulfil a long-suppressed death wish. He wrote to Marsh that he had not joined the army for patriotic reasons.

Rosenberg's life in the army was unutterably wretched. He wrote to Lascelles Abercrombie on 11 March 1916: 'the army is the most detestable invention on this earth and nobody but a private in the army knows what it is to be a slave' (*Collected Works*, p. 230). On 26 January 1918, in a passage cancelled by the censor, he wrote to Edward Marsh: 'what is happening to me now is more tragic than the "passion play." Christ never endured what I endure. It is breaking me completely.'[2] Everything conspired to make Rosenberg's army life a long nightmare. He detested the coarseness of his fellow soldiers' behaviour and the crudity of their minds. His lot was worsened by the anti-Jewish prejudice that he encountered among officers and private soldiers alike. Because the boots issued by the army did not fit him, he suffered the agony of sore heels, not nearly as trivial a matter as civilians at home might reckon. His awkwardness, stubbornness, and forgetfulness must have made matters worse: he was punished for leaving behind his gas mask, and the injustice of army discipline rankled with him. The continual labour that was his lot imposed severe strains on his physique. Dragging heavy coils of barbed wire into no-man's-land and setting them up, or digging latrines in the hard earth or in the excremental mud, weighed upon his body and his spirit. He refers several times to the

[2]From an unpublished letter quoted in J. Cohen, *Journey to the Trenches* (London, 1975), p. 3.

difficulty of writing and of perfecting his poems in such conditions. The lives of officers were at least as dangerous as those of their men, but they enjoyed some compensations. They had the services of a batman, who would keep their uniform clean; their food and sleeping quarters were better; they were exempt from physical labour and from punishments such as pack drill for trivial breaches of discipline; they could afford to relax in decent hotels and restaurants on short leaves instead of in the bistros where private soldiers congregated; they might even make the acquaintance of cultivated Belgian or French civilians; and with luck they would find one or two congenial fellow officers in their regiment or company.

It is probably true that Rosenberg never met in the army a single person who cared for any of the arts or with whom he could have the kind of talk that meant so much to him. One of his officers, Frank Waley, asked Rosenberg for copies of some of his poems. Rosenberg was always short of paper, being obliged to write some poems on the backs of envelopes; neverthless he gave Waley a few poems that baffled him so completely that he chucked them away. The only one Waley could remember was 'Break of Day in the Trenches,' and since he didn't think it was poetry, he threw it out with the rest.

In 1916, at his own expense, Rosenberg published in a volume entitled *Moses* an unfinished play of that name, together with some shorter poems. It is convenient to group it with another play, *The Unicorn*, a work of only a few pages, completed in the summer of 1917, although in March 1918 he was planning to write a fuller treatment of the play, which he had always regarded as a sketch for a larger version.

Although only 470 lines long, *Moses* is an extremely complex work about whose significance there is still no general agreement. Rosenberg wrote to the poet R. C. Trevelyan in a letter postmarked 15 June 1916: 'Moses symbolizes the fierce desire for virility, and original action in contrast to slavery of the most abject kind' (*Collected Works*, p. 235). Knowing Rosenberg's views about the slavery of private soldiers, one is entitled to say that *Moses* presents Rosenberg's situation in 1915–1916. It also marks the culminating stage in his rejection of the divinity whom he had scrutinized in a number of poems and stigmatized in 'God' as 'the miasma of a rotting God.' ('This miasma of a rotting god' also occurs as line 144 of *Moses*). One may also read the play as Rosenberg's attempt to define the historical destiny of the Jews and of the proletariat. It expresses his preoccupation with violence as a force that may possibly regenerate a crumbling, sick society, a notion that he had played with even before the outbreak of war. The only overt act of violence occurs at the end of the play, when Moses strangles the brutal Egyptian overseer, Abinoah, father of his mistress, Koelue. She may also stand for the incarnate sexuality of the earth goddess whom Rosenberg had long envisaged as the supplanter of the orthodox male God.

The Unicorn is even shorter and stranger than *Moses*. It is about a decaying race who have never seen a woman, and whose chief, named Tel, is mounted on a unicorn. The two other main characters, Saul and his wife, Lilith, belong to another tribe, as does Enoch, the only other character. The climax of the play is best described in the final stage direction:

Through the casement they see riding under the rainbow a black naked host on various animals, the Unicorn leading. A woman is clasped on every one, some are frantic, others white or unconscious, some nestle laughing. ENOCH with madness in his eyes leaps through the casement and disappears with a splash in the well. SAUL leaps after him shouting 'The Unicorn.' TEL places the unconscious LILITH on the Unicorn and they all ride away.

(*Collected Works*, p. 173)

In a letter to Winifreda Seaton dated 8 March 1918 Rosenberg wrote of his ambitions for an expanded version of *The Unicorn*: 'I mean to put all my innermost experiences into the 'Unicorn.' I want it to symbolize the war and all the devastating forces, let loose by an ambitious and unscrupulous will' (*Collected Works*, p. 270).

Some of the themes of *Moses* reappear in *The Unicorn*, notably those of sexuality and violence as the instruments of liberation and change. Before starting work on the fragments that became *The Unicorn* Rosenberg had contemplated writing a play about Judas Maccabeus, who reconquered Jerusalem from the Romans in 165 B.C. He may also have had in mind a quotation from the Book of Numbers: 'God brought them out of Egypt; he hath as it were the strength of a unicorn.'

It is the richness and complexity of the themes and the way in which they mirror Rosenberg's psychological turmoil that constitute the fascination of these plays, whether one ranks them among his greatest achievements or regards them as only partially successful despite their imaginative force and the magnificent passages of verse found in them.

Although Rosenberg was a mature artist by the outbreak of war and had written some hauntingly original poems by early 1916, it is on a handful of poems written between spring 1916 and his death on 1 April 1918 that his reputation securely rests. He wrote to Edward Marsh on 4 August 1916, enclosing 'A Worm Fed on the Heart of Corinth' and 'Break of Day in the Trenches.' The former prophesies, in ten astonishing lines, the destruction of England by a creature akin to the invisible worm of William Blake's 'The Sick Rose.' With this poem Rosenberg takes his place among the Hebrew prophets and the English poets. 'Break of Day in the Trenches,' actually written in the trenches, is a flawless, ironical meditation, that opens with an ominous strangeness:

The darkness crumbles away.
It is the same old druid Time as ever.

In his letter to Marsh, Rosenberg observes: 'I am enclosing a poem I wrote in the trenches, which is surely as simple as ordinary talk. You might object to the second line as vague, but that was the best way I could express the sense of dawn' (*Collected Works*, p. 239). The sight of a rat that leaps over the poet's hand as he plucks a poppy to stick behind his ear moves him to meditate sardonically on the rat's cosmopolitan sympathies, which lead him to touch first an English, next a German, hand. He then imagines the rat's grin as he watches men in all their bodily pride reduced to short-lived creatures with terror in their eyes. At the very end of the poem the image of the poppy returns.

The poppy held great emotional potency for the soldiers in France and Flanders: indeed Englishmen still wear paper poppies in their buttonholes on Armistice Day. John McCrae, a Canadian, wrote the most popular poem of the war, 'In Flanders Fields,' which begins:

In Flanders fields the poppies blow
Between the crosses, row on row.

The first half of McCrae's poem is reasonably competent versifying, although the second half represents a sad decline. But Rosenberg has made the symbol of the plucked poppy ironically resonant with our sense of life's brevity and of the mortality that is the lot of rat and poppy and men:

Poppies whose roots are in man's veins
Drop, and are ever dropping;
But mine in my ear is safe—
Just a little white with the dust.

('Break of Day in the
Trenches,' 23–26)

In May 1917, Rosenberg sent Marsh a seventy-nine-line poem, 'Dead Man's Dump,' based on his own experience of carrying wire up to the line on limbers and running over dead bodies. It contains Rosenberg's only realistic descriptions of the battlefield, yet his main concern is still his search for the meaning of human existence, his desire to discover the metaphysical significance of war. He is capable of writing lines that convey with horrifying exactness the sensation of driving a cart over dead bodies:

The wheels lurched over sprawled dead
But pained them not, though their bones crunched.

(7–8)

The poem ends in a similar vein, but at the middle of it the

52

sight of the dead moves Rosenberg to compose a passage unrivaled in any other poem of the war, except in Wilfred Owen's finest work:

None saw their spirits' shadow shake the grass,
Or stood aside for the half used life to pass
Out of those doomed nostrils and the doomed mouth,
When the swift iron burning bee
Drained the wild honey of their youth.

(27–31)

The imagery here of honey and iron occurs also in 'August 1914,' a beautiful short lyric written in the summer of 1916.

Two further poems of 1917 show Rosenberg's imagination at its strangest and most potent. 'Daughters of War' evokes mysterious Amazons whose lovers are soldiers killed in battle and washed clean of mortal dust. He believed it to be his best poem, and during the year that he spent on it he had 'striven to get that sense of inexorableness the human (or inhuman) side of this war has' (*Collected Works*, p. 260).

Again, in 'Returning, We Hear the Larks,' Rosenberg explores in this brief lyric themes to which he continually recurs: war, beauty, sexuality, the menacing power of women. The lark song that at first brings only joy carries a sombre reminder:

Death could drop from the dark
As easily as song—
But song only dropped,
Like a blind man's dreams on the sand
By dangerous tides,
Like a girl's dark hair for she dreams no ruins lie there,
Or her kisses where a serpent hides.

(10–16)

Rosenberg continued to write poems of high quality until a few days before his death. In a letter to Marsh dated 28 March 1918 he enclosed his last poem, 'Through These Pale Cold Days,' the third of three meditations on Jewish history and Jewish destiny. On 30 and 31 March Rosenberg's regiment suffered heavy casualities while resisting the German advance, and in the early hours of the morning on 1 April his company was making its way back in order to gain a brief respite from the fighting. Rosenberg volunteered to return to the battle and within an hour was killed in close combat near the French village of Fampoux.

WHAT THE SOLDIERS SANG

The British army sang on the march, in trenches, in billets, in bistros, and in concert halls. The songs that gave strength and comfort to the troops are often ignored by literary critics, who have failed to recognize in them the most considerable body of poetry in English composed and sung by the common man.

Not all the songs were anonymous products of the trenches,. 'Tipperary,' arguably the most famous of marching songs, although the troops came to loathe it, was written in 1912 by a professional composer. 'Keep the Home Fires Burning,' which belongs to 1915–1916 and the march to the Somme, brought fame and money to the youthful Ivor Novello, who after 1918 wrote, acted in, and directed a long series of spectacular musical comedies at Drury Lane.

Yet the overwhelming majority of trench songs were by anonymous soldiers. Some of them may have been written by one man for performance at a concert, before being adopted, embroidered, or parodied by troops in different parts of the line. Others may have been the work of soldiers, put together during a rest period and then transmitted by word of mouth to men of other regiments. A few songs, some of which went back to the eighteenth and nineteenth centuries, were inherited from the pre-1914 regular army.

The words sung with such gusto were often parodies of well-known hymns, ballads, and musical comedy and music-hall songs: they were usually fitted to existing tunes, sacred and profane. The authors of these songs, whoever the may have been, portrayed themselves as cowardly, lecherous, sceptical of victory, disrespectful toward their military superiors, unappreciative of the charms or the morals of French women such as 'Mademoiselle from Armenteers,' longing only to get back to England. 'I Don't Want to Die' begins:

I want to go home,
I want to go home,
I don't want to go to the trenches no more,
Where whizz-bangs and shrapnel they whistle and roar.

That inglorious declaration finds a parallel in 'I Don't Want to Be a Soldier,' a parody of 'On Sunday I Walk Out with a Soldier,' a song of the kind loathed by Sassoon, which was sung in a revue, *The Passing Show of 1914*, produced at the London Hippodrome:

I don't want to be a soldier,
I don't want to go to war.
I'd rather stay at home,
Around the streets to roam,
And live on the earnings of well-paid whore.

Not all the songs referred to the war. 'Wash Me in the Water,' widely sung throughout the war, seems to bear no relevance to the fighting, probably because it is said to have been sung by the regular army before 1914. It was set to a Salvation Army hymn tune:

Wash me in the water
That you washed your dirty daughter
And I shall be whiter
Than the whitewash on the wall.

When no officers were present, 'your dirty daughter' might become 'the colonel's daughter.'

But almost all the finest songs have deep roots in the daily lives of those who composed and sang them. 'The Old Barbed Wire' provides a superb example of the way in which contemptuous humour, apparent callousness, and deadly accuracy combine to make an unforgettable song:

If you want to find the sergeant,
I know where he is, I know where he is,
If you want to find the sergeant,

I know where he is,
He's lying on the canteen floor.

The quarter-bloke (the quartermaster sergeant) is miles
behind the line; the sergeant-major is boozing up the
privates' rum; the CO is down in the deep dugouts. Then
comes the final dramatic twist:

If you want to find the old battalion,
I know where they are, I know where they are.
If you want to find the old battalion,
I know where they are,
They're hanging on the old barbed wire.

In 1963 Joan Littlewood's musical extravaganza *Oh What
a Lovely War* made brilliant use of these songs; yet it
would be wrong to think of them merely as part of a
theatrical entertainment. They commemorate, more
fittingly than the headstones of the Imperial War Graves
Commission, the lives and deaths of those gallant though
unheroic common soldiers who, when the noise of the
guns had died down, were found lying in the mud or
hanging on the old barbed wire.

THE AFTERMATH:
HERBERT READ AND DAVID JONES

In the early 1920's and during the rest of the decade,
English novelists tried to give order and coherence to
their experience and memories of the war by writing prose
fiction. No poet of any merit essayed this task by means
of his art until the next decade. There then appeared two
poems of some length, *The End of a War* (1933) by
Herbert Read and *In Parenthesis* (1937) by David Jones.
Neither can be described as a novel in verse or even as an
orthodox narrative poem, yet both attempt to assimilate
certain qualities of modern prose fiction and to build
something less impressionistic and lyrical than the war
poems that we have considered in this essay.

Herbert Read (1893–1968) fought with distinction in
the war, earning the Distinguished Service Order and the

Military Cross. His book of poems *Songs of Chaos* (1915) was followed by a second, *Naked Warriors* (1919). Although Read was to enjoy a long career as a literary critic and aesthetician, he had not in 1919 seen any of those works by Antonio Pollaiuolo or other Florentine painters conjured up by the book's title, whose progenitor is almost certainly Wordsworth's 'Character of a Happy Warrior,' a poem that is a source book of high-minded schoolmasters and of politicians eager to sanctify their wartime speeches with an edifying quotation from a great poet:

Who is the happy Warrior? Who is he
That every man in arms should wish to be?

Read gives his answer to Wordsworth's query of 1805:

Bloody saliva
Dribbles down his shapeless jacket.

I saw him stab
And stab again
A well-killed Boche.

This is the happy warrior,
This is he . . .

(6–12)

'The Execution of Cornelius Vane' anatomizes the life and death of a soldier who shoots away his right index finger and works thereafter in a cookhouse. Required to fight in an emergency, he points to his mutilated hand that cannot fire a rifle, only to be told by a sergeant, 'But you can stab.' Vane deserts, is tried by court-martial, and is sentenced to death. His executioners, men of his own regiment looking very sad, blindfold him, and just before he is shot he says to the assembly:

'What wrong have I done that I should leave these:
The bright sun rising
And the birds that sing?'

(130–132)

'Kneeshaw Goes to War' analyzes a soldier whose passivity and failure to respond to the world of experience

57

are perhaps more ignoble than Vane's cowardice. He loses a leg in battle and, after returning to England, accepts after long meditation the need to live by the truth and to discipline oneself. The poem anticipates, in its probing of a man's inner life, the intricate analysis of character found in Read's *The End of a War*.'

Read's poetry is almost invariably marked by cool intelligence and firm restraint. Very occasionally he permits his emotion to speak nakedly and movingly; such a moment occurs in 'My Company':

But, God! I know that I'll stand
Someday in the loneliest wilderness,

I know that I'll wander with a cry:
'O beautiful men, O men I loved,
O whither are you gone, my company?'

(26–27; 32–34)

It is this kind of passion, this kind of rhythmical vitality, that one finds wanting in Read's most ambitious poem, *The End of a War*.

The poem comprises three interwoven monologues: 'Meditation of the Dying German Officer,' 'Dialogue Between Body and Soul,' and 'Meditation of the Waking English Officer.' The prose Argument summarizes the main incident of the poem (it can hardly be called the main action, for it is an almost wholly static poem). Briefly, on 10 November 1918 a wounded German officer tells a British officer that a village nearby is undefended. German machine-gunners hidden in the church tower fire on the British battalion resting in the village square, killing or wounding a hundred men. The survivors bayonet the hidden machine-gunners and a corporal dispatches the German officer, who dies impassively. Later, the British find the dismembered body of a French girl who had been raped and tortured by the Germans. The English officer falls asleep, exhausted and nauseated. When he wakes in the morning the church bells are ringing in the armistice.

Despite the grandeur of his theme, Read fails to give his poem life, and the characters are only mouthpieces through whom the poet utters his leaden, monochrome soliloquies. The language remains so inert that even the armistice bells cannot stir it into activity. Extensive quotation would not substantiate that judgment, because the reader might suspect that the hostile critic had picked out the worst passages to prove his case. Here is a short extract, which shows Read in a comparatively sprightly mood, taken from the English officer's meditation:

> ... First there are the dead to bury
> O God, the dead. How can God's bell
> ring out from that unholy ambush?
> That tower of death! In excess of horror
> war died.
>
> (26–30)

The reader must discover for himself whether that extract is representative of Read's poem.

The End of a War is a praiseworthy attempt to confront some philosophical questions that have pre-occupied thoughtful men and women for centuries: the existence of God, the significance of war and violence in society, the limits of political obligation. Yet although the poem has won critical acclaim during the past half-century, it can rank only as an honorable failure. One suspects that *The End of a War* has been more often referred to than read, and more frequently read than enjoyed.

David Jones (1895–1974) was, like Isaac Rosenberg, both poet and painter. He was educated at Camberwell Art School from 1909 to 1914 and enlisted in the Royal Welch Fusiliers, serving at the front as a private soldier from December 1915 to March 1918. He became a convert to Roman Catholicism in 1921 and lived by his painting until the mid-1930's, thereafter dividing his time between his work as painter, engraver, and typographer, and his work as a writer.

In Parenthesis, begun in 1928 and published in 1937, could be described as an epic in verse about World War I, although it is unlike traditional epic, contains long passages of prose, and celebrates wars much older than the conflict of 1914–1918. It is an extremely difficult, highly allusive poem, although Jones provides thirty-five pages of notes designed, unlike those of *The Waste Land*, to elucidate rather than to tantalize. Yet even the notes offer a formidable array of theological speculation, assorted myth, army jargon, and references to historical events.

Jones sets his poem between early December 1915 and early July 1916, telling us in the preface that after the Somme battle everything became more impersonal, mechanical, and relentless. He could not have written *In Parenthesis* about the mass slaughter that characterized the war after the midsummer of 1916.

The story concerns a battalion in an infantry camp in England preparing to embark for France. It lands in France and makes it way by stages to the trenches, these preliminary movements being completed on Christmas Day 1915. The opening three sections of the poem are followed by three sections that describe a typical day in the trenches and the southward marches toward the Somme. The final section concentrates on the part played in the disastrous Somme offensive of July 1916 by Number 7 platoon, under the command of Lieutenant Jenkins. We follow in particular one of its members, Private Ball, who is indeed the sole survivor of the attack. The poem ends, after the nightmare of battle, with the garlanding of the dead by a figure from Jones's private mythology, the Queen of the Woods, who is in part the goddess Diana and in part the dryad of folklore.

The poem is difficult for a variety of reasons: Jones has at his fingertips and within his imagination a wealth of allusions drawn from heterogeneous and complex sources, of which the principal are Roman history, the Gospels, the so-called Matter of Britain (the Arthurian legends), the whole Romano-Celtic tradition, early English and medieval literature, and the rites of the Roman Catholic Church, especially the Mass. Jones attempts to fuse the raw material of the epic with the technique employed in a modernist poem such as *The Waste Land*, wherein the impressionistic use of imagery and evocative incantation of rhythm largely supersede the formal logic of argument and the orderly unfolding of narrative.

Yet behind these highly elaborate literary devices one senses the presence of the private soldiers with their routine blasphemies, their cockney speech, and their daily suffering. Nor must one forget Jones's constant sardonic humour. Even Private John Ball, hero of the epic tale (insofar as there is one), is so called not only because his namesake was the priest who led the Peasants' Revolt in 1381. As John Stallworthy observes in his *Survivors' Songs in Welsh Poetry* (1982), Ball's name has a further significance: coming after that of Private Leg in the sergeant's roster, and following the last two digits, 01, in his army number, it is both ballistic and anatomical.

When Private Ball lies wounded he finally abandons his rifle, even though he remembers the admonitions of the instructors in musketry:

Marry it man! Marry it!
Cherish her, she's your very own.
   Coax it man coax it – it's delicately and
      ingeniously made
—it's an instrument of precision – it costs us tax-payers
money – I want you men to remember that.

(pp. 183–184)

That might well come from a work of naturalistic fiction, yet it coexists with the boast of Dai-Great-Coat, uttered after the men of Number 1 Section have shared a meager benefit of bread and rum. In his lengthy boast Dai, a character in Thomas Malory's *Morte Darthur*, who stands here for the private soldier throughout the ages, claims to have participated in all kinds of historical and mythical events involving the use of hand weapons from the war in Heaven onward:

I served Longinus that Dux bait-blind and bent;
   the dandy Xth are my regiment;
who diced
Crown and Mud-hook
under the Tree, . . .

(p. 83)

This is a fairly simple example of Jones's elaborate allusiveness. The Xth Fretensis is reputed to have furnished the escort party at Jesus' crucifixion, and the dicing under the Cross is equated with the gambling game Crown and Mud-hook, or Crown and Anchor, that was popular among the troops in World War I. Jones's repeated collocation of exalted moments from the past with the brutal or trivial events of the war is not designed to glorify the war or, indeed, to diminish the splendour of history and legend. He wants us to apprehend the timelessness of human action. In a later poem, 'The Fatigue,' he imagines that the execution of Christ is carried out not by the Xth Fretensis but by a party of British soldiers of World War I.

The prose of *In Parenthesis* ranges from the demotic to the hieratic, the brutally simple to the densely allusive. The verse covers an equally wide gamut of form and of emotional resonance. The closing pages of the poem attain a climax of rare poetic intensity, when the Queen of the Woods comes to deck with garlands all who have died in the battle, officers and other ranks, the loved and the detested, German and British alike. Nothing in the poetry of the war excels this luminous requiem:

> For Balder she reaches high to fetch his.
> Ulrich smiles for his myrtle wand.
> That swine Lillywhite has daisies to his chain – you'd
>   hardly credit it.
> She plaits torques of equal splendour for Mr. Jenkins and
>   Billy Crower.
> Hansel with Goronwy share dog-violets for a palm, where
>   they lie in serious embrace beneath the twisted tripod.
>
> (p. 185)

Jones ends *In Parenthesis* with René Hague's translation of lines from the *Chanson de Roland*:

> The geste says this and the man who was on the field . . . and who wrote the book . . . the man who does not know this has not understood anything.
>
> (p. 187)

Those words may serve as an epitaph for the poets of

1914–1918, whether they appear in the pages of this essay or not, and as a commemoration of all who suffered and bore witness on the battlefields of World War I.

WAR POETS 1914–1918

A Select Bibliography

(Place of publication London, unless stated otherwise)

Note: Select bibliographies of Robert Graves and of Wilfred Owen are appended to the essays on these writers in the present series.

Anthologies

GEORGIAN POETRY, ed. E. Marsh (1911–12, 1913–15, 1916–17, 1918–19, 1920–2).

AN ANTHOLOGY OF WAR POEMS, ed. L. Brereton (1930).

—with an Introduction by E. Blunden.

AN ANTHOLOGY OF WAR POETRY, ed. R. Nichols (1943).

—contains a long Introduction in the form of a dialogue between Nichols and J. Tennyson.

UP THE LINE TO DEATH: THE WAR POETS 1914–1918, ed. B. Gardner (1964).

—with an Introductory Note by E. Blunden.

MEN WHO MARCH AWAY: POEMS OF THE FIRST WORLD WAR, ed. with an Introduction by I. M. Parsons (1965).

THE LONG TRAIL: WHAT THE BRITISH SOLDIER SANG AND SAID IN THE GREAT WAR OF 1914–18, ed. J. Brophy and E. Partridge (1965).

—revised and rewritten edn. of *Songs and Slang of the British Soldier 1914–18*, 1938.

POETRY OF THE FIRST WORLD WAR, sel. and ed. M. Hussey (1967).

THE PENGUIN BOOK OF FIRST WORLD WAR POETRY, ed. J. Silkin; Harmondsworth (1981).

LAURENCE BINYON

Collected Works:

THE FOUR YEARS: WAR POEMS (1919).

COLLECTED POEMS, 2 vols. (1931).

Separate Works:

THE ANVIL (1916).

THE CAUSE: POEMS OF THE WAR (1917).

FOR THE FALLEN (1917).

EDMUND BLUNDEN

Bibliography:

A BIBLIOGRAPHY OF EDMUND BLUNDEN, by B. J. Kirkpatrick; Oxford (1979).

Collected Works:

POEMS, 1914–1930 (1930).

EDMUND BLUNDEN: A SELECTION OF HIS POETRY AND PROSE, ed. K. Hopkins (1950).

POEMS OF MANY YEARS (1956).

—with a Preface by Blunden.

SELECTED POEMS, ed. R. Marsack; Manchester (1982).

Separate Works:

UNDERTONES OF WAR (1928). *Verse and Prose.*

WAR POETS 1914–1918 (1958). *Criticism.*

Critical Studies:

EDMUND BLUNDEN, by A. M. Hardie (1958).

—revised edn. 1971.

THE POETRY OF EDMUND BLUNDEN, by M. Thorpe (1971).

RUPERT BROOKE

Bibliography:

A BIBLIOGRAPHY, by G. Keynes (1954).

Collected Works:

COLLECTED POEMS: WITH A MEMOIR BY EDWARD MARSH (1918).

THE POETICAL WORKS, ed. G. Keynes (1946).

THE PROSE, ed. C. Hassall (1956).

LETTERS, ed. G. Keynes (1968).

Separate Works:

POEMS (1911).

1914 AND OTHER POEMS (1915).

JOHN WEBSTER AND THE ELIZABETHAN DRAMA (1916).

LETTERS FROM AMERICA, with a Preface by H. James (1916).

Critical Studies:

RUPERT BROOKE AND THE INTELLECTUAL IMAGINATION, by W. de la Mare (1919).

RECOLLECTIONS OF RUPERT BROOKE, by M. Browne (1927).

RED WINE OF YOUTH: A LIFE OF R. BROOKE, by A. J. A. Stringer; Indianapolis (1948).

RUPERT BROOKE, by C. Hassall (1964).

THE HANDSOMEST YOUNG MAN IN ENGLAND: RUPERT BROOKE, by M. Hastings (1967).

—lavishly illustrated.

RUPERT BROOKE: DRAFTS AND FAIR COPIES IN THE AUTHOR'S HAND (1974).
—with a Foreword and Introduction by G. Keynes.

FORD MADOX FORD
Collected Works:
COLLECTED POEMS; New York (1936).

JULIAN GRENFELL
Separate Works:
BATTLE; Flanders (1915).
Critical Studies:
JULIAN GRENFELL, by V. Meynell (1917).
—a memoir with poems.
JULIAN GRENFELL, by N. Mosley (1976).
—based on Grenfell family papers.

IVOR GURNEY
Collected Works.
POEMS BY IVOR GURNEY (1954).
—with a Memoir by E. Blunden.
POEMS OF IVOR GURNEY 1890–1937 (1973).
—with an Introduction by E. Blunden and a Bibliographical Note by L. Clark.
COLLECTED POEMS OF IVOR GURNEY, edited and with an Introduction by P. J. Kavanagh (1982).
—the first major collection of Gurney's work. It includes over 300 poems, of which more than 100 have not previously been collected.
WAR LETTERS OF IVOR GURNEY, sel. and ed. by R. K. R. Thornton; Manchester (1983).
Separate Works:
SEVERN AND SOMME (1917).
WAR'S EMBERS, AND OTHER VERSES (1919).
Critical Studies:
THE ORDEAL OF IVOR GURNEY, by M. Hurd (1978).

W. N. HODGSON
Collected Works:
VERSE AND PROSE IN PEACE AND WAR (1917).

A. E. HOUSMAN
Collected Works:
COLLECTED POEMS (1939).

DAVID JONES
Collected Works:
DAVID JONES: LETTERS TO VERNON WATKINS, ed. R. Pryor; Cardiff (1976).

DAI GREATCOAT: A SELF-PORTRAIT OF DAVID JONES IN HIS LETTERS, ed. R. Hague (1980).

INTRODUCING DAVID JONES: A SELECTION OF HIS WRITINGS, ed. J. Matthias (1980).

Separate Works:
IN PARENTHESIS (1937). *Verse and prose.*

THE ANATHEMATA: FRAGMENTS OF AN ATTEMPTED WRITING (1952). *Verse and prose.*

EPOCH AND ARTIST: SELECTED WRITINGS, ed. H. Grisewood (1959). *Prose.*

THE SLEEPING LORD AND OTHER FRAGMENTS (1974). *Verse and prose.*

—although these later writings do not have as their theme the First World War, they all throw light upon *In Parenthesis.*

Critical Studies:
DAVID JONES: ARTIST AND WRITER by D. Blamires; Manchester (1971).

DAVID JONES, by R. Hague; Cardiff (1975).

DAVID JONES: AN EXPLORATORY STUDY OF THE WRITINGS, by J. Hooker (1975).

DAVID JONES: EIGHT ESSAYS ON HIS WORK AS WRITER AND ARTIST, ed. R. Mathias; Llandysul (1976).

DAVID JONES, by S. Rees; New York (1978).

THE LONG CONVERSATION: A MEMOIR OF DAVID JONES, by W. Blissett (1981).

ROBERT NICHOLS
Collected Works:
SUCH WAS MY SINGING: A SELECTION FROM POEMS 1915–1940 (1942).

Separate Works:
    INVOCATION: WAR POEMS AND OTHERS (1915).
    ARDOURS AND ENDURANCES (1917).
    AN ANTHOLOGY OF WAR POETRY ed. R. Nichols (1943).
    —contains a long Introduction in the form of a dialogue between Nichols and J. Tennyson.

HERBERT READ

Collected Works:
    COLLECTED POEMS (1966).
Separate Works:
    SONGS OF CHAOS (1915). *Verse.*
    NAKED WARRIORS (1919). *Verse.*
    IN RETREAT (1925). *Prose Narrative.*
    AMBUSH (1930). *Prose Narrative.*
    THE END OF A WAR (1933). *Verse.*
Critical Studies:
    HERBERT READ by F. Berry (1961).

ISAAC ROSENBERG

Collected Works:
    POEMS, ed. G. Bottomley (1922).
    —with a Memoir by L. Binyon.
    COLLECTED WORKS, ed. G. Bottomley and D. Harding (1937), with a Foreword by S. Sassoon.
    —poems, prose, letters and drawings.
    COLLECTED POEMS, ed. G. Bottomley and D. Harding (1949).
    COLLECTED WORKS, ed. with an Introduction and Notes by I. Parsons and a Foreword by S. Sassoon.
    —the 1937 edition, revised and enlarged.
Critical Studies:
    JOURNEY TO THE TRENCHES: THE LIFE OF ISAAC ROSENBERG, 1890–1918, by J. Cohen (1975).
    ISAAC ROSENBERG: THE HALF-USED LIFE, by J. Liddiard (1975).
    ISAAC ROSENBERG: POET AND PAINTER, by J. M. Wilson (1975).

Note: The catalogues of two Exhibitions contain valuable

material on Rosenberg. The first is *Isaac Rosenberg 1890–1918: Catalogue with Letters,* ed. M. de Sausmarez and J. Silkin, Leeds University Exhibition Catalogue, Leeds, 1959. The second is the National Book League Exhibition Catalogue, ed. J. Liddiard and C. Simmons, London, 1978.

SIEGFRIED SASSOON
Bibliography
A BIBLIOGRAPHY, by G. Keynes (1962).
Collected Works:
THE WAR POEMS (1919).
THE COMPLETE MEMOIRS OF GEORGE SHERSTON (1937). *Prose.*
—includes *Memoirs of a Fox-Hunting Man, Memoirs of an Infantry Officer,* and *Sherston's Progress.*
COLLECTED POEMS (1947).
COLLECTED POEMS 1908–56 (1961).
SELECTED POEMS (1968).
—paper back edition.
THE WAR POEMS, arranged and introduced by R. Hart-Davies (1983).
—with Sassoon's explanatory notes.
Separate Works:
THE OLD HUNTSMAN AND OTHER POEMS (1917). *Verse.*
COUNTER-ATTACK AND OTHER POEMS (1918). *Verse.*
PICTURE SHOW; Cambridge (1919). *Verse.*
SATIRICAL POEMS (1926). *Verse.*
—with additional poems, 1933.
THE HEART'S JOURNEY (1927). *Verse.*
MEMOIRS OF A FUX-HUNTING MAN (1928). *Memoirs.*
MEMOIRS OF AN INFANTRY OFFICER (1931). *Memoirs.*
SHERSTON'S PROGRESS (1936). *Memoirs.*
THE OLD CENTURY AND SEVEN MORE YEARS (1938). *Memoirs.*
—reprinted in paperback edition with introduction by M. Thorpe, 1968.
THE WEALD OF YOUTH (1942). *Memoirs.*
SIEGFRIED'S JOURNEY, 1916–1920 (1945). *Memoirs.*
DIARIES 1920–1922, ed. and introduced by R. Hart-Davis (1982).
DIARIES 1915–1918, ed. R. Hart-Davis (1983).
Critical Studies:
SIEGFRIED SASSOON: A CRITICAL STUDY, by M. Thorpe (1966).

CHARLES SORLEY
Collected Works:
MARLBOROUGH AND OTHER POEMS; Cambridge (1916).
—5th edition revised and enlarged, 1922.
LETTERS FROM GERMANY; Cambridge (1916).
THE LETTERS WITH A CHAPTER OF BIOGRAPHY; Cambridge (1919).
Critical Studies:
THE UNGIRT RUNNER: CHARLES HAMILTON SORLEY, POET OF WORLD WAR I, by T. B. Swann; Hamden, Conn. (1965).

EDWARD THOMAS
Collected Works:
COLLECTED POEMS (1920).
COLLECTED POEMS, ed. R. G. Thomas (1978).
—the definitive edition, with an elaborate critical apparatus.
LETTERS FROM EDWARD THOMAS TO GORDON BOTTOMLEY, ed. R. G. Thomas (1958).
Critical Studies:
AS IT WAS, by Helen Thomas (1926).
WORLD WITHOUT END, by Helen Thomas (1931).
—an account of her life with Edward by his widow. The two volumes are obtainable in a single volume.
THE LIFE AND LETTERS OF EDWARD THOMAS, by J. Moore (1939).
EDWARD THOMAS, by H. Coombes (1956).
EDWARD THOMAS: THE LAST FOUR YEARS, by E. Farjeon (1958).
EDWARD THOMAS, by V. Scannell (1965).
EDWARD THOMAS: A CRITICAL BIOGRAPHY, by W. Cooke (1970).
EDWARD THOMAS, by A. Motion (1980).

A. G. WEST
Separate Works:
THE DIARY OF A DEAD OFFICER; BEING THE POSTHUMOUS PAPERS OF ARTHUR GRAEME WEST (1918).
—edited with an introduction by C. J. (C. E. M. Joad).
General Criticism:
WAR POETS 1914–1918, by E. Blunden (1958).

ENGLISH POETRY OF THE FIRST WORLD WAR, by J. H. Johnston (1964).
—a detailed study of the leading poets of the war.
HEROES' TWILIGHT: A STUDY OF THE LITERATURE OF THE GREAT WAR, by B. Bergonzi (1965).
OUT OF BATTLE: THE POETRY OF THE GREAT WAR, by J. Silkin (1972).
—contains long, thoughtful studies of the leading poets of the war.
POETS OF THE FIRST WORLD WAR, by J. Stallworthy (1974).
THE GREAT WAR AND MODERN MEMORY, by P. Fussell (1975).

LIST OF WORKS CONSULTED

ASQUITH, H.
Poems 1912–33, Sidgwick and Jackson, 1934.
BINYON, L.
The Four Years, Elkin Matthews, 1919.
BLUNDEN, E.
Poems of Many Years, Collins, 1957.
War Poets 1914–1918, Longman, 1958
BROOKE, R.
The Poetical Works, Faber, 1946.
BROPHY, J. and PARTRIDGE, E.
The Long Trail, Deutsch, 1965.
—all songs in the section What the Soldiers Sang
COHEN, J.
Journey to the Trenches, Robson Books, 1975.
FORD, F. M.
Collected Poems, Oxford University Press, New York, 1936.
GURNEY, I.
Poems by Ivor Gurney, Hutchinson, 1954.
Poems of Ivor Gurney, Chatto and Windus, 1973.
HASSALL, C.
Rupert Brooke, Faber, 1964.
—quotation from a letter by Edward Thomas.
HODGSON, W. N.
Verse and Prose in Peace and War, Murray, 1917.
HOUSMAN, A. E.
Collected Poems, Cape, 1939.

JOLLIFFE, J.
  Raymond Asquith, Collins, 1980.
JONES, D.
  In Parenthesis, Faber, 1963.
MOSLEY, N.
  Julian Grenfell, Weidenfeld, 1976.
  —all verse and prose by Grenfell.
NICHOLS, R.
  Ardours and Endurances, Chatto and Windus, 1917.
READ, H.
  Collected Poems, Faber, 1966.
ROSENBERG, I.
  Collected Works, Chatto and Windus, 1979.
SASSOON, S.
  Collected Poems 1908–56, Faber, 1961.
SHAW-STEWART, P.
  'I saw a man this morning' – text from Up the Line to Death,
  ed. B. Gardner, Methuen, 1964.
SORLEY, C.
  Marlborough and Other Poems, Cambridge University
  Press, 1922.
  Letters, Cambridge University Press, 1919.
THOMAS, E.
  Collected Poems, Faber, 1978.
WEST, A.G.
  The Diary of a Dead Officer, Allen and Unwin, 1918.